Marie Hodge

Strategies and Skills for

MANAGERIAL WOMEN

Johanna Hunsaker, Ph.D.

Associate Professor of
Organizational Behavior
University of San Diego

Phillip Hunsaker, D.B.A.

Professor of Management
Director of Management Programs
University of San Diego

G85

Published by

SOUTH-WESTERN PUBLISHING CO.

CINCINNATI   WEST CHICAGO, IL   DALLAS   PELHAM MANOR, NY   LIVERMORE, CA

CONTENTS

iii

CHAPTER 5.   MANAGING YOURSELF

CHAPTER 6.   DEVELOPING EFFECTIVE
COMMUNICATION SKILLS

CHAPTER 7.   HANDLING POWER AND POLITICS

CHAPTER 8.   WORKING EFFECTIVELY WITH GROUPS

CHAPTER 9.   DEALING WITH DIFFICULT EMPLOYEES

PREFACE

In our management classes at the University of San Diego, we have watched the proportion of female students change dramatically. Only ten years ago it was a rarity to find more than a handful of females in the business school. This has changed in the 1980s. Today there are roughly equal proportions of males and females in our classrooms. Social and legal changes have brought this about, along with an increasing awareness of the number of options available to both males and females in modern society. Women are continuing to move into the world of work in increasing numbers. As they gain confidence in their abilities, they seek opportunities to move into managerial positions.

We have noticed a phenomenon among our female students that prompted us, in part, to write this book. In our undergraduate courses, when task groups are formed to complete class projects, male students emerge as group leaders over 75 percent of the time. We have observed this same phenomenon when conducting basic management seminars for new first-line supervisors in industrial, educational, and governmental settings. However, a different story emerges at the graduate level when we look at the behavior of students in our MBA classes and when we observe the behavior of women in upper managerial ranks who have "made it." There is a marked difference in the degree of leadership exhibited. In this case, women emerge just as often as men in leadership roles.

One of the factors which contributes to women's increased leadership effectiveness at the graduate level and in upper-level management is that their experiences and skills are different. They have "overcome" many of the negative aspects of the female socialization process. They have had experiences interacting with others as supervisors in real-life organizational settings. They have developed a managerial frame of mind and have utilized managerial skills. They have gained confidence in their own credibility and are effective leaders.

If you plan to use this book to launch or enhance your managerial career, remember the following points. First of all, you already have the drive and ambition required to accomplish your goals; otherwise, you wouldn't be reading this right now. You are also aware that you need additional skills to succeed, and obviously you are willing to invest your time to develop them. This type of attitude, motivation, and awareness on your part means that you are halfway there already. You can now read on about the unique problems and opportunities awaiting you, and you will soon be developing the essential management skills necessary to aid you in achieving your personal and career goals.

Purpose

The purpose of this book is to provide new women managers and supervisors, or those aspiring to managerial positions, with the fundamental skills and insights necessary for success. This book is addressed to women who hope to be in management, to those women in management who want to move ahead, and to those who simply want to become more knowledgeable, skilled, and effective. Many of the managerial skills presented here are the same skills required of any successful manager—male or female. It is important to recognize, however, that women must simultaneously deal with other problems, such as role conflict, dual careers, and lack of acceptance, which make the acquisition and application of these skills more difficult. Our goal is that, with your dedication, this book can enhance your career in management as well as your personal life.

Organization of the Book

A key contribution of this book is that it highlights the many unique problems that confront female managers but not their male counterparts. As you read through Chapter 1, you will become more aware of limiting stereotypes, attitudes, and behaviors—those posed by both women themselves and the external environment. The strategies presented for dealing with them and changing them will be of immediate benefit to any reader, male or female. This book is action-oriented; that is, we expect you to take the skills presented and develop your own individualized strategies for improving yourself and your career.

Part of the strategy for success is mastering the functions of management discussed in Chapter 2. But it takes more than academic competence to achieve success in management. Equally important are the strategies for projecting a positive image which are presented in Chapter 3; the ways to find and maintain relationships with a mentor which are explained in Chapter 4; and the determination to master your own life by coping with stress, managing your time, and developing your career as discussed in Chapter 5. Throughout this book we have quoted from successful women managers, many of whom have their pictures on various pages, who have reported that these strategies have enhanced their careers, and even their personal lives.

Because a managerial job is people-intensive, you will have to work on your communication skills as suggested in Chapter 6. In addition, you should realize that power and politics in organizational life are a reality. Traditionally women have suffered several power failures. You should be able to strengthen your base of influence immediately by applying some of the strategies for acquiring personal power presented in Chapter 7.

A popular definition of management is that it is the "art of getting things done through people." This means that you should know how to delegate and be familiar with the key group processes discussed in Chapter 8. In Chapter 9 we explain how to deal effectively with difficult employees, especially in conflict situations. Finally, in Chapter 10 we present skills you will need when you hire or fire your own employees.

The Epilogue provides a brief review of the book, allows you to assess yourself on the various skills and attitudes discussed in the first ten chapters, and suggests a plan to follow in changing yourself for success.

Instructor's Manual

For each of the ten chapters in this book, there are teaching suggestions, two or more practical exercises, some suggested films, objective and essay questions, and transparency masters. This Instructor's Manual (Stock No. G85M) is available free of charge to instructors who adopt this book for class use.

Acknowledgments

Many people contribute to an effort such as this, and we would like to acknowledge and thank those who helped to make this book possible. We appreciate the comments of Dr. Margaret Fenn, University of Washington, Seattle; and Dr. Mary Giovannini, Northeast Missouri State University, who both reviewed the manuscript. In addition, we would like to thank the following individuals for providing research resources and a supportive environment: Jim Burns, Dean, School of Business Administration, University of San Diego; Ed De Roche, Dean, School of Education, University of San Diego; and Art Traynor, research assistant, University of San Diego. And thanks to our daughter Sarah, who endured many days and evenings of the writing process.

Finally, because this book is about women managers, we owe a debt of gratitude to the many female students who have helped refine our ideas and strategies and to the women who attend our seminars. Your insights and experiences have influenced us profoundly.

Johanna S. Hunsaker
Phillip L. Hunsaker

CHAPTER 1

Making the Move to Management

OUTLINE

I. Barriers Between Doing and Managing

   A. Traditional Socialization Process for Women
   B. Pressures of Female Sex Roles

      1. Mother
      2. Seductress
      3. Pet
      4. Iron Maiden

   C. The "Queen Bee" Syndrome

II. Our Historically Sexist Society

   A. Role Models Provided Since Birth
   B. Role Constraints
   C. Myths and Stereotypes—and Realities

      1. Stereotype #1. Men Are Intellectually Superior to Women
      2. Stereotype #2. Men Value Achievements and Meaningful Work More than Women
      3. Stereotype #3. Men Are Inherently More Assertive than Women
      4. Stereotype #4. Women Don't Work for Money

III. Overcoming of Outdated Conceptions

Now that a number of career women have become media celebrities, many people think that women in management experience nothing but nonstop glamour. According to Foxworth, moving into management is sometimes celebrated as becoming "queen of the corporation."[1] Situated in a luxurious office with a reception area filled with admiring male vice-presidents, the sparkling female executive looks forward to returning home to an approving husband or friend and a chilled bottle of champagne and gourmet dinner he prepared himself.

What a disappointment to discover that the spectacular successes of a chosen few have been so overplayed by the media! Realistic, everyday living and working experiences do not usually match up with what the media portray. The sad truth is that management is still pretty much male territory. If women expect to get into management—and especially if they stay there—they will have to learn their way around it, usually through the school of hard knocks. Of course, women managers need to develop the same skills and insights that new male managers must acquire, but women are new immigrants to a world of customs and language in which men have been raised all along. Since men also realize this, women must, in addition, prove themselves as "naturalized citizens" as well as competent managers.

According to Stewart, the appearance of a *new* woman manager produces neither instant credibility nor instant alarm, but an attitude of "Let's wait and see."[2] Reactions to new female managers are much more open-minded than they have been in the past, and this receptiveness is accompanied with suspended judgment allowing women the chance to demonstrate their abilities.

Current managers, both male and female, will be seeking answers to unexpressed questions about how the new female manager will affect their own well-being and that of the organization. Does she really have managerial skills? Does she have the emotional makeup to handle the pressure and responsibilities of the job? Will this new environment throw her, or can she assimilate it and fit in appropriately?

Women entering management positions straight out of graduate or undergraduate business school programs have a headstart in acculturation. They have had two to four years of working with males in academic settings where they learned and got accustomed to business language, which often consists of male-oriented analogies and parallels. "Game playing," "team member," and "playing hardball" are all common workday terms with which they would be familiar. They also have gained experience in working successfully in male-dominated task groups.

For women reentering the job market after a long absence or those born before World War II who are venturing into it for the first time, the greater cultural shock makes the already stressful new management job even more complicated. Such an experience can result in anything—from a momentary annoyance for those adequately prepared to a devastating emotional jolt for those entering cold. If a wounded ego, disappointment, or bewilderment shows through, it may reinforce any existing negative stereotypes and mark the new woman manager as being "bad" for company morale and a negative influence on other employees. Consequently, it's important for her to "roll with the punches," and learn the "game rules" as quickly as possible. This chapter will cover some of the difficulties many women encounter when making the move from subordinates to managers.

BARRIERS BETWEEN DOING AND MANAGING

The critical shift is from "doing" to "managing." Women have traditionally been *doers*, with specific job descriptions like typists or computer programmers. The results of their efforts have usually been readily observable in terms of documents typed or programs operating. A high degree of security has been provided in their clear-cut responsibilities, behaviors, and tangible feedback available.

As *managers*, women are responsible for accomplishing tasks with and through other people. Consequently, there is no longer a clear-cut definition of performance, outcome, or the reward process. Now the essential variables are more ambiguous. It is not always clear what needs to be done to motivate others, how to measure results, or how to spend time effectively at any given moment. Work such as planning and evaluation is not tangible; and the security of performing mixed, routine tasks has changed to a game of chance—with big risks, but also big rewards.

Traditional Socialization Process for Women

Some of the dimensions of the socialization process discussed in this chapter present barriers to women in making the transition to management. As pointed out by Fenn, female roles usually require short, discrete time intervals that provide a *time orientation* useful for reacting to and solving specific human needs.[3] In management, however, longer time orientations are needed for activities such as goal setting and planning.

A second difference in women's socialization is that most of them do not have the experience of playing in group sports that men do. The argument suggests that understanding and practice in *collaborative team efforts* are important in developing leadership and supportive work environments. Boys learn early that it is necessary to cooperate with others whom they may not particularly like in order to have a winning team. Girls place higher emphasis on friendships. According to Hennig and Jardim, girls are more apt to refuse playing games with those they don't like.[4] This carries over into organizational life when women fail to understand that personal likes and dislikes are *irrelevant* in making the team effective. Colwill has argued more recently that, while the team-sport-organization analogy had some intuitive appeal, there is a lack of any real evidence to support this theory.[5]

Most women in organizations are still far from the managerial ranks. A prominent feature of most female occupations, according to Colwill, is that of **helpmate**: assisting others in their work.[6] Typical examples are nurse, secretary, receptionist, etc. This type of position fosters helplessness and dependency which are the antithesis of the qualities needed in managers.

Pressures of Female Sex Roles

Even when a woman does finally break through into the managerial ranks, she may find that she is the only female manager in her company. If this happens, the male majority may actively pressure her into a female sex role. A common set of *female roles*, discussed below, have been described by Kanter.[7]

Mother. The female manager sometimes finds that she has become a "mother" to a group of male subordinates. They bring their troubles to her and she comforts them. This role is based on the stereotyped assumption that women are nurturing and sympathetic listeners. The consequences of being typecast in a mother role are that: (1) the role is relatively safe from sexual harassment; (2) the "mother" becomes an emotional specialist rather than a task-oriented leader, and this perpetrates a traditional stereotype; (3) the "mother" is rewarded by men for services rendered, rather than for independent leadership.

Seductress. The dangerous element of sexual competition can interfere with the female manager's effectiveness if she is cast as a sex object by male subordinates, peers, or superiors. If the female manager is typecast as a "seductress" who shares her attentions with many admirers, she may be debased. If, on the other hand, she forms a close alliance with one particular man, she may arouse resentment from the others. If a high-status male becomes her "protector," the seductress may be resented for "using her body" to get an "in" with superiors. Although a seductress is rewarded with attention, she experiences much tension and her perceived sexuality interferes with all other characteristics which are now more important for the job and career.

Pet. The **pet** is a token role where the female is symbolically included in the group like a mascot or cheerleader, but not as an equal or influential figure. She is tolerated more as a cute, amusing novelty than as a competent peer or manager. On the positive side, at least the woman is included in the male-dominated group. On the other hand, she is prevented from demonstrating and developing her managerial competence.

Iron Maiden. If the new woman manager resists falling into any of the three roles just mentioned, and persists in acting in a task-oriented manner, she often is typecast as the tough, "women's libber" type—the **iron maiden.** This may occur by her simply demanding equal treatment because, in the particular male-dominated setting, no woman has ever done that before. By displaying competence and cutting off sexual innuendoes, she may be seen as threatening to her male counterparts and this could cause resentment and suspicion. Consequently, even behaving in healthy, self-actualizing ways can elicit a male response which traps women in more militant roles than they prefer.

Although these roles differ greatly, they all are forms of differentiating women as inconsequential minorities. All these roles indicate that this is a "woman," not a "competent manager." These roles isolate women from the mainstream and diminish their potential effectiveness.

The "Queen Bee" Syndrome

The **Queen Bee**, according to Colwill, is a successful woman who has made it to the top by working harder than most men, and "will be damned if she's going to reach down and help some other woman on the climb."[8] The Queen Bee attempts to close the boardroom doors behind her and keep her hard-earned and well-deserved privileges for herself. If another woman is allowed to approach this lofty perch, it will be through the "I had to suffer, so you will too" syndrome.

OUR HISTORICALLY SEXIST SOCIETY

Long before little girls and boys grow up to become the victims and the perpetrators of gender-related stereotypes, subtle influences are at work. Very early in their lives children learn about sex roles. They learn these roles through relatively simple patterns that most of us take for granted. Parents throw baby boys up in the air and roughhouse with them. They coo over baby girls and handle them delicately. From the earliest days they choose gender-related colors and toys for their children. They encourage the energy and physical activity of their sons, just as they expect their daughters to be more quiet, docile, and ladylike. And though they love their sons and daughters with equal fervor, many people are disappointed when there is no male child to carry on the family name.

When children enter school, the pattern continues. From the moment children pick up their first book, they are given the message that boys are competent, active, and adventuresome while girls are bungling, inept, dependent, and dumb—capable only of doing domestic chores or making themselves attractive. In many *old-edition* textbooks, boys are consistently portrayed as being able to ride a rocketship to the moon or perform delicate surgery, while girls are shown almost exclusively baking cakes, doing laundry, helping or watching boys.

By the time men and women enter the workplace, they have been immersed in a sexist society. They have come to hold beliefs about themselves, the world, and the people in it. Some of the views have come consciously, others unconsciously. They come from parents, teachers, media, and advertising—almost every facet of society.

These common cultural stereotypes lead to many of the problems the woman manager encounters when she enters the world of work. By examining the socialization process, a better understanding of the role constraints, myths, and stereotypes that may hinder women can be developed.

Role Models Provided Since Birth

People are socialized from birth to fit the traditional role models provided for them. And the roles provided have been very different for little boys and little girls. Most aspects of traditional child rearing have an impact on later behavior—in particular, aggressive versus passive behaviors, views on competition, the effects of labeling, and the individual's perception of his or her ability to succeed.

As children, certain types of behavior are rewarded or punished, not necessarily overtly, but by subtle clues from both parents. When children are at age 4 or 5, they generally become more aggressive toward their environment. For a little boy, aggression means playing with toys such as guns and cars, roughhousing with Dad, and playing competitive ball games. His aggressive, competitive behavior is usually supported, encouraged, and rewarded by both parents. At this early age he is taught that aggressive behavior is acceptable to his parents (as representatives of the larger society) and that he should strive to actively manipulate his environment.

On the other hand, usually the 5-year-old girl receives her

rewards from both parents for acting in a more quiet way. Playing with dolls, cooking, and other types of behavior that model her mother may be reinforced. She is not usually found wrestling on the floor with Dad, out playing catch with him, or playing cowboys and Indians. Most fathers typically reward a 4- or 5-year-old daughter by giving her love and attention in return for her relinquishment of aggressive behavior. She understands from subtle cues which behavior is not "ladylike" and, for fear of losing her mother's love, she may choose to identify with her mother to please both parents.

Hennig and Jardim, in their classic book *The Managerial Woman*, hold that the socialization differences described above result in males being able to use aggression constructively, whereas females are socialized to be weak and subordinate.[9] They explain that boys are more valued by society for their active engagement with their environment while girls, receiving different cues from both parents, learn passivity as an expectation and acquire a "second-class citizen" stature. Boys also learn, through their childhood activities, to believe more in their own ability to control fate (and outcomes), whereas girls are given little opportunity to experiment with situations in which initiative and risk are required.

The child's actual play also affects the self-image. Recently much has been written about team sports as an outlet for male aggression and, more importantly, as a way of learning the rules of competition. Males participate in team sports from as early as age 5 and learn that winning and losing are both acceptable. Soccer, football, and baseball provide a way of learning cooperation and competition, specialization, leadership, how to handle criticism, and the need for alternative plans and goals.

Most women over age 30 today were not encouraged as children to participate in team sports. When they were 5-year-olds, they engaged in activities which were seen as feminine—such as taking ballet lessons and helping Mom in the kitchen—and as more acceptable to society. What most of these women have missed when growing up has been the opportunity to learn a sophisticated manipulation of their environment: how to win or lose, and the rules of game playing. Not having had exposure to comfortable competition, most of them have had to compete on another level—physical appearance. Winning or losing has become an entirely different experience, tied to less intellectual pursuits.

Fortunately, today some things have changed. Some soccer teams with elementary-age children now have girls on them, for example. Although seemingly insignificant, these types of changes will go a long way in breaking down the traditonal male/female roles in the socialization process. They cannot, however, help the adult woman who is beginning her managerial career burdened with traditional strategies.

Society, through its process of socialization, has viewed masculinity as synonymous with strength, dominance, and power and has reinforced the male's attitudes regarding his own powers. Simultaneously, it has reinforced the female's feelings of weakness, inadequacy, and lack of control over her environment.

Role Constraints

The socialization process leads to role constraints: "What I *must* do because I am a Male/Female. What I *cannot* do because I am a Female/Male." These role constraints often lead to assumptions about what behaviors are appropriate and desirable for members of each sex. Choosing to depart from traditional male/female roles involves shedding old values and adopting new ones. This is easier to talk about than to do.

Not too long ago we conducted an informal experiment with graduate students enrolled in an MBA program. We thought perhaps this group of people might not feel as constrained by their gender as the average person. We asked the students to complete a questionnaire including the following unfinished sentences:

"Because I am a female ...."
"Because I am a male ...."

The responses revealed the overwhelming impact of the socialization process and the widespread existence of gender-related role constraints. Here are some typical answers:

1. Because I am a female, I am still trying to develop my career outside of my home—mainly because I felt my

responsibility to my family comes first.

2. Because I am a female, men find it hard to accept my intelligence and aggressive attitude. Oftentimes I'm forced to role-play a passive person in order to get something that I want instead of being able to be my true self. Men can't handle being less smart than a woman.

3. Because I am a male, I feel compelled to be a success in every endeavor I take on.

4. Because I am a male, I feel obligated to be protective toward women and small children; also, to be responsible for the more important decisions made.

These comments show the effects of socialization and subsequent role constraints. A summary of the comments gathered is illustrated in Figure 1-1. These data demonstrate that constraints are felt by both men and women as a result of their socialization process.

FIGURE 1-1

SUMMARY OF RESPONSES ON ROLE CONSTRAINTS

Because I am a male . . .

I must be successful.
I must be the dominant figure.
I have more responsibilities; I must go to school and get a good education; I must be competitive.
I feel strong and determined.
I must wear the pants in the family.
I must take care of my wife financially.
I must dominate.
I can be rowdy and crude.
I can't cry in public.
I must be aggressive.
I have unlimited freedom.

Because I am a female . . .

I must be responsible to family first.
I must play passive.
I can't play competitive sports.
I am emotional.
I have role restrictions.
I have barriers to what I want.
I must accept the roles of today and make the most of it.
I find it hard to get into the good "old boys' network."
I must be cautious of my behavior.
I had stricter rules as a child.
I can cry to get my own way.

Myths and Stereotypes—and Realities

There is little systematic information upon which to base assumptions of differential managerial ability between sexes. Most "known" differences are based on stereotypes. **Stereotypes** are *assumed* differences, social conventions or norms, learned behaviors, attitudes, and expectations. Stereotyping simplifies the perceptual process by allowing us to evaluate an individual or a thing on the basis of our perception of the group or class to which he, she, or it belongs.

Sex-role stereotyping is a major complication for women aspiring to, or currently in, management. A sampling of the widely accepted notions about women and work include:

- Women cannot coordinate careers with family demands.
- Women cry in crisis situations.
- Women are not suited emotionally or intellectually for jobs traditionally held by men.
- Women are not committed to their jobs and regard jobs as temporary measures.
- Women cannot travel for business.

According to Pickford, because these and countless other myths and stereotypes are "based on fears, desires, needs, and emotions—not reality—it is all the more powerful against the facts refuting it."[10] Dispelling these deeply ingrained attitudes and associated social pressures is difficult.

Some of the common stereotypes which impede women's progress in the work force need closer scrutiny. The perpetuation of the following stereotypes has limited many a woman's drive to seek managerial positions.

Stereotype #1. Men Are Intellectually Superior to Women. Research comparing men and women on aptitude tests does not support this view. The research shows that females, in general, achieve well in their early school years. They do not differ from males in intellectual abilities, methods of learning, creativity, or cognitive style. The most consistent finding is that women surpass men on tests of verbal aptitude. Young girls tend to excel in tests of memory and in scholastic achievement. However, this achievement tends to diminish as they reach adolescence and adulthood. Nevertheless, scholastic achievement and femininity are not incongruent.

The stereotype of the ideal woman discourages her expression of intellectual abilities, however. Hollander found that, when the grade point average of high school males increased, their self-esteem also increased; whereas the self-esteem of females *decreased* with increases in grade point average.[11]

The net result of the perpetuation of this outmoded stereotype is that the woman manager is often torn between the desire for approval and the need to achieve and demonstrate her competence. Most women managers have had to make concessions that men have not had to make, and these concessions have lessened the expression of their competence. A confrontation between men with conflicting ideas is usually perceived as "healthy and natural." The same behavior by women, on the other hand, might be viewed as "aggressive and bitchy."

Stereotype #2. Men Value Achievements and Meaningful Work More than Women. Research indicates that women value and are motivated by many of the same job elements as men. Bruning and Snyder found that both males and females have similar job characteristic-preferences-commitment and find intrinsic satisfaction to be more important than extrinsic motivators.[12] In other words, the work itself was what satisfied both the women and men. There were no differences between the sexes in the expressed importance of the intrinsic factor.

Additional research has elaborated on the similarities between male and female managers. Donnell and Hall found that male and female managers have no significant differences in their managerial style.[13] Renwick discovered that men and women have similar attitudes toward conflict resolution.[14] Brief and Oliver revealed that women have the same feelings about work as men.[15] Finally, Birdsall found that male and female managers' communication style with subordinates was basically the same.[16]

Despite these similarities, several studies have highlighted some critical differences that have undoubtedly handicapped women in their quest to convince companies of their knowledge and abilities. First, some research demonstrates that women have traditionally had a self-image problem. For example, Prather found that women are not too often taken seriously as people.[17] As a result, they tend to have low self-esteem. Low self-esteem combined with a low self-image can be crippling.

Fear of success is another problem women face. Dowling labeled the fear of success the **Cinderella complex**.[18] She described the tendency of some women to sabotage their careers because of the fear that, if they are *too* successful, they won't appeal to "Prince Charming."

Women often self-select themselves away from certain types of jobs. Heinen *et al.* found that many women having high achievement levels traditionally channeled this need in socially acceptable ways.[19] This usually meant getting into jobs they perceived as "female" jobs like nursing and teaching. These fit nicely into the roles for which girls were socialized—and which threatened no one. This viewpoint, however, leads to problems for the woman pursuing a traditionally "male" career.

In corporate life this traditional view presents the aspiring woman with a double-edged sword. Taking on the "male" traits and attributes needed for a management role may leave her feeling somehow less feminine and more dominant and aggressive than she and others are comfortable with. If she fails to demonstrate these qualities, however, she will not even merit consideration for the position, let alone advancement up the organizational ladder.

These required behaviors often conflict with the desired self-image and contribute to a fear of success. Many women are reluctant to enter the management field since they may view the requisites for successful performance as being inconsistent with their self-image. They view success as unfeminine and therefore undesirable. Hull stated that the biggest barrier to female success is insecurity.[20]

Men, already established in managerial roles, do not usually help resolve this conflict. Often, with the entry of women into leadership positions, they fear losing power, authority, control, and identity. The role of protector and provider enforced in their childhood is now threatened. In addition, competition will be keener for the dwindling number of top management jobs. Stanek says that, with women in the running, there will be twice as many able, hard-working, and dedicated top managers to choose from.[21]

It is important to note, however, that women's role in our society is rapidly changing and the old rules may not be applicable for long. Koff and Handlon, after a six-year study into the factors causing success or failure of women in management positions, discovered that successful women view achievement as female-appropriate behavior.[22] They found that while many women with low self-esteem fall into the "stay-put prone" group because of fear of failure, disloyalty to a peer group, or conflict with tradition, other women are high achievers and can be described as "pioneers." This latter group expect to be successful. They are willing to take risks and their strong upwardly-mobile motivations are made possible, in part, by their very positive sense of self-worth.

For older or noncollege-educated women, success in managerial roles may still require some rethinking of an appropriate self-image. But as more and more women enter the work force and have successful careers, the image should change to a positive one. Currently, females make up 40 to 50 percent of the undergraduate and graduate business school enrollments. This equal career socialization and preparation may do much to eliminate the traditional conflict between positive self-image and career success, which is especially troublesome for women managers.

Stereotype #3. Men Are Inherently More Assertive than Women. The "ideal" stereotypes of the aggressive, driving male and the sweet, passive female are well-known. In fact, American women do generally tend to score lower than men on personality measures of dominance. However, the argument can be made that this is because of cultural values rather than a basic biological difference.

Heinen *et al.* found that cultural conditioning tends to cause women to hide negative feelings such as hostility or aggressiveness.[23] When facing conflict, most women tend to "run away" or attempt to smooth over hostile feelings between people. For this reason, managing conflict can be particularly difficult for them. Alpander and Guttman found the tendency toward a "relationship" orientation by women not wholly surprising.[24] It has been customarily accepted that women in the working world are more aware of, and concerned about, the human interrelationships in a working group than men. This is possibly due to their "family orientation" and "caring" instincts.

This tendency of women to be more relationship-oriented should not be viewed as a deficit, however. Effective leadership requires both task- and relationship-oriented behaviors. Men, traditionally, have been high on task but low on relationship dimensions. This was one reason why sensitivity training caught on so well in the business world. On the other hand, research on female leadership, according to Heinen *et al.*, indicates that women can assimilate and learn the task roles requiring influence and assertiveness.[25] An example of this phenomenon is the current popularity of assertiveness training seminars for women. Carr-Ruffino advocates the rule: *Go directly to the persons involved.*[26] She argues that women can become comfortable with behaving assertively in work situations. With proper "reconditioning," both men and women can become proficient in the task and relationship roles required for effective management.

Stereotype #4. Women Don't Work for Money. According to recent U. S. Department of Labor statistics, 53 percent of all women over age 16 are in the paid labor force, and of these most work because of economic need.[27] Many women *want* to work, but a large percentage of them work because they are the sole support for either themselves or their families. For married couples, it is frequently the wife's earnings that are responsible for raising joint income above the poverty level.

The current economy strains even high-income households and is devastating to middle-class and poor families. The divorce rate in the United States has climbed since 1960, and families headed by females make up a staggering 48 percent of all families living in poverty. As a result, 9 out of 10 women join the workforce at some time in their lives—for 25 years on the average if they are married, 45 years if they are single. However, they are invariably clustered at the bottom of the occupational ladder—earning 63 cents for every dollar a man earns.[28]

In addition to the economic motivation of coping with today's economy, which highlights the necessity of more women working for money, our survey indicated other reasons why women enter the labor force. One woman manager rebutted this stereotype most eloquently:

I'm amazed when it is assumed that women are not

interested in, or motivated by, money. We women learn early that money and power go hand in hand. We observed our mothers and have ourselves been in positions of having to ask for money or being allocated a certain sum for household and personal use. Money probably has more importance to us than to the average male, who is accustomed to producing and controlling it.

The ultimate dire consequence of sex-role stereotypes is that they may become self-fulfilling. Women who have been taught most of their lives to be passive, ladylike, dependent, cooperative, and accepting have come to either believe in these notions or struggle with the conflict of not believing them, but not being able to disprove them. Men in our society also believe most of these notions. What is set in motion, as a result of these traits ascribed to women, is the following self-fulfilling prophecy: "If everyone (society) sees me as passive, or lacking the ability to control my life, then I must be that way for society tells me what I am. I will then act in ways to confirm those images, for that is what is expected."

In summary, most of today's women, from early childhood, acquired a socialized role (that of wife and mother) with accompanying behaviors and images of appropriateness for that role. Faced with entry into a "work" organization, they believe that success is good as long as it doesn't interfere with their feminine role and does not threaten what they have come to see as the "more superior" male.

OVERCOMING OF OUTDATED CONCEPTIONS

Faced with the realities of the psychological, social, and organizational barriers, one has to wonder, "Is there a future for women in management?"

The answer is yes. A look at demographics provides an appreciation that opportunities do and will continue to exist. More women than ever before are in the labor force, and they continue to enter the managerial ranks at growing rates. Women's opportunity to enter at the lower management ranks has increased significantly in this century. In 1900, 3 percent of management positions were held by women; in 1950, 12 percent; in 1980, 26 percent; and in 1983, 33 percent. The number of women at the highest level of corporate management is still relatively small, as Table 1-1 shows.[29]

TABLE 1-1

WOMEN'S PARTICIPATION IN MANAGEMENT POSITIONS, 1900-1983

	1900	1950	1980	1983
Management positions— Supervisor through top manager	3%	12%	26%	33%
Top-management positions	0%	0.4%	5%	5%

Several conditions contribute to the increase of women in management positions: longer life expectancy, smaller families, rising educational levels, and economic necessity. Many other factors enhance the eligibility of, and need for, women in managerial roles. These include:

1. A shift from product to service businesses in the American economy.

2. Changes in family roles and in public attitudes.

3. Increasing employment opportunities in managerial positions due to organizational growth, branching, and decentralization.

4. Changing values and life-styles.

5. Legal requirements for nondiscrimination, equal opportunity, and equal pay.

There is a need for both individuals and organizations, however, to reexamine stereotypes and distorted perceptions if women are to adapt and take advantage of existing opportunities. The primary responsibility, however, is with aspiring women managers themselves. After all, they bear the primary responsibility for their own career success. How they manage their own careers will have an impact on changing their organizations and on overcoming outdated conceptions.

Keeping in mind this process, two very basic assumptions about both men and women can help. They are:

1. Human beings have the ultimate choice of creating and acting on alternatives.

2. Human beings need to be true to themselves, *even* if it means not "fitting" into society.

Women accepting these assumptions will have a better chance at breaking both visible and invisible barriers than those who rely on outdated conceptions and stereotypes to mold their lives. If women have accepted these assumptions, they are ready for the subject of the next chapter—the "basics" that are essential to performing successfully as a manager.

FOOTNOTES

1. J. Foxworth, "They're Still the New Kids on the Block," *Prime Time* (October, 1981), pp. 50-55.

2. N. Stewart, *The Effective Woman Manager* (New York: John Wiley & Sons, 1978), p. 2.

3. Margaret Fenn, *Making It in Management: A Behavioral Approach for Women Executives* (Englewood Cliffs, NJ: Prentice-Hall, 1978), p. 46.

4. Margaret Hennig and Anne Jardim, *The Managerial Woman* (New York: Pocket Books, 1978).

5. Nina Colwill, *The New Partnership: Women and Men in Organizations* (Palo Alto, CA: Mayfield Publishing Co., 1982), p. 41.

6. *Ibid.*, p. 26.

7. R. Kanter, "Women in Organizations: Sex Roles, Group Dynamics, and Change Strategies," in A. Sargent (ed.), *Beyond Sex Roles* (St. Paul: West Publishing Co., 1977).

8. Colwill, *op. cit.*, pp. 43-44.

9. Hennig and Jardim, *op. cit.*, pp. 76-81.

10. L. J. Pickford, "The Superstructure of Myths Supporting the Subordination of Women," in B. A. Stead, *Women in Management* (Englewood Cliffs, NJ: Prentice-Hall, 1985), pp. 165-174.

11. J. Hollander, "Sex Differences in Sources of Social Esteem," *Journal of Consulting and Clinical Psychology*, 38 (1972), pp. 343-47.

12. N. Bruning and R. Snyder, "Sex and Position as Predictors of Organizational Commitment," *Academy of Management Journal*, 26 (1983), pp. 485-491. See also S. D. Saleh and M. Lalljee, "Sex and Job Orientation," *Personnel Psychology*, Vol. 22 (1969), pp. 465-471.

13. S. Donnell and J. Hall, "Men and Women as Managers: A Significant Case of No Significant Difference," *Organizational Dynamics*, 8 (1980), pp. 60-77.

14. P. A. Renwick, "The Effects of Sex Differences on the Perception and Management of Superior-Subordinate Conflict: An Exploratory Study," *Organizational Behavior and Human Performance*, 19 (1977), pp. 403-415.

15. A. P. Brief and R. L. Oliver, "Male-Female Differences in Work Attitudes Among Retail Sales Managers," *Journal of Applied Psychology* (1976), pp. 526-528.

16. D. Birdsall, "A Comparative Analysis of Male and Female Managerial Communication Style in Two Organizations," *Journal of Vocational Behavior*, 16 (1980), pp. 183-196.

17. Jane Prather, "Why Can't Women Be More Like Men—A Summary of the Sociopsychological Factors Hindering Women's Advancement in the Professions," *American Behavioral Scientist*, 15 (1971), pp. 172-182.

18. Colette Dowling, *The Cinderella Complex* (New York: Simon and Schuster, 1981).

19. J. Stephen Heinen *et al.*, "Developing the Woman Manager," *Personnel Journal* (May, 1975), pp. 282-289.

20. J. B. Hull, "Female Bosses Say Biggest Barriers Are Insecurity and Being a Woman," *Savvy* (Nov. 2, 1982).

21. Lou W. Stanek, "Women in Management: Can It Be a Renaissance for Everybody?" *Management Review* (November, 1980), pp. 44-48.

22. Lois A. Koff and Joseph H. Handlon, "Women in Management: Keys to Success or Failure," *Personnel Administrator* (April, 1975), pp. 24-28.

23. Heinen, *et al.*, *op. cit.*

24. G. G. Alpander and J. E. Guttman, "Contents and Techniques of Management Development Programs for Women," *Personnel Journal* (February, 1976), pp. 26-79.

25. Heinen, *et al.*, *op. cit.*

26. Norma Carr-Ruffino, *The Promotable Woman* (Belmont, CA: Wadsworth Publishing Co., 1985), pp. 168-169.

27. U.S. Department of Labor, Bureau of Labor Statistics, *Employment and Earnings* (January, 1983).

28. U.S. Department of Commerce, Bureau of Census, *Money Income of Households, Families, and Persons in the U.S.*, Series P-60, No. 142 (1984).

29. U.S. Department of Labor, Bureau of Labor Statistics, *Employment and Earnings* (January, 1984).

CHAPTER 2

Assuming Managerial Roles and Functions

<u>OUTLINE</u>

I. A Manager's Wide Range of Roles

   A. A Manager Assumes Responsibility
   B. A Manager Must Balance Competing Goals
   C. A Manager Must Be a Conceptual Thinker
   D. A Manager Must Be Problem Oriented
   E. A Manager Works with and Through Other People
   F. A Manager Is a Mediator
   G. A Manager Is a Politician
   H. A Manager Is a Diplomat
   I. A Manager Makes Difficult Decisions

II. Functions of Management

   A. Planning

      1. Women as Planners
      2. Planning Aids
      3. Evaluation of Planning Effectiveness

   B. Organizing

      1. Women as Organizers
      2. Organizing Aids

   C. Staffing

      1. The Staffing Process
      2. Women and Staffing

   D. Leading

      1. Women as Leaders
      2. Leadership Aids
      3. Task and Relationship Behaviors

   E. Controlling

      1. Women as Controllers
      2. Controlling Aids

III. Variations of the Managerial Processes
Action Guidelines

   A. Avoid Traditional Female Roles

   B. Clarify Your Managerial Role Expectations

   C. Become Proficient in the Functions of Management

Having obtained a managerial position, it is important to measure up to expectations in order to keep the position and to move on to positions of greater responsibility. Important questions include: What does the organization expect of a manager in terms of performance? What are the main elements of managing? What are the manager's responsibilities as a leader? This chapter will provide women with strategies for successfully establishing credibility as managers. The first step is a clear understanding of the manager's job. This is diagrammed in Figure 2-1.

A MANAGER'S WIDE RANGE OF ROLES

Essentially, the manager's job is to make efficient and effective use of the organization's resources, such as people, time, money, technology, machinery, and information, to accomplish the organization's goals. Managers at every level are deputized to do this within their own unique area of responsibility. The organization provides the specific goals, policies, operating systems, personnel, and other physical resources. The manager is entrusted to make decisions and produce the desired results leading to organizational goal accomplishment. The manager accomplishes these objectives through the functions of planning, organizing, staffing, leading, and controlling, which will be discussed in depth later. In performing these managerial functions, however, a manager will assume a wide range of roles in order to be effective. Stoner has provided the following summary of a manager's myriad roles:[1]

A Manager Assumes Responsibility

Managers are in charge of specific tasks and must see to it that they are done successfully. In fact, successful task accomplishment is the primary basis for evaluating managerial performance. In addition, managers are responsible for the actions of their subordinates. *The success or failure of subordinates is a direct indication of managerial effectiveness.* Consequently, it is important to put aside personal feelings towards subordinates and build a cooperative and supportive task team.

FIGURE 2-1

THE MANAGER'S JOB

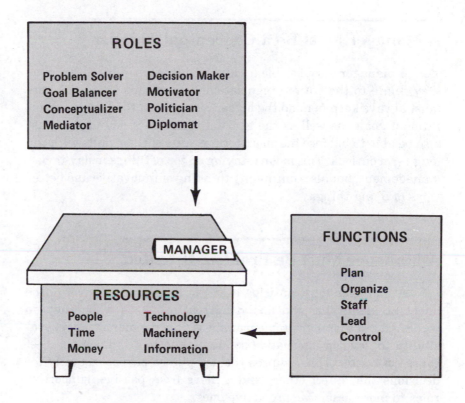

A Manager Must Balance Competing Goals

Because organizational resources are limited, a manager must strike a balance between the organization's various goals and needs. One strategy is to arrange each day's tasks in order of priority. It helps to do those things that need to be done right away, and relegate to a lower priority those that can be done later. The effective use of time (a manager's most valuable resource) is discussed in Chapter 5.

A manager must also decide *who* is to perform each particular task based on each subordinate's area of expertise and the various projects that need to be accomplished. This requires analytical skills and assertive behaviors which a manager may not have developed in previous nonsupervisory positions.

A Manager Must Be a Conceptual Thinker

A manager must be able to think about tasks in the abstract as they relate to the entire organization. This means that managers must always keep in mind the bigger picture, i.e., the larger organizational goals, as well as the goals of their units. Managers must also be able to balance the short-term results of their units with the long-term outlook. This means staying on top of things in day-to-day management, but also continually thinking of innovative and better ways of doing things.

A Manager Must Be Problem-Oriented

A manager must anticipate extraordinary situations and be adept at identifying and analyzing real problems when they do occur. After a thorough problem analysis, it is the manager's responsibility to develop alternative solutions and to decide on the best course of action. This requires the acceptance of responsibility for decisions that affect others and a move from passive, supportive roles to more assertive, pro-active ones.

A Manager Works with and Through Other People

New managers quickly learn that in order to do an effective job as a manager, it is necessary to rely not only on their own subordinates and supervisors, but also on their peers and other staff members in the organization. This means it is important to reinforce working relationships upward, downward, and laterally within the organization. Managers act as channels of communication in all these directions within the organization.

A Manager Is a Mediator

Since organizations are made up of people with differing needs and values, disagreements often occur. Conflict can provide opportunities for growth and creativity. Disagreements can also have negative effects on morale and productivity if they are not managed appropriately. Although no manager wants disruptive conflicts to occur, oftentimes these conflicts do arise. It then becomes the manager's responsibility to act in the role of mediator in order to resolve these disagreements before they get out of control. New managers who move from women's traditional "doer" roles which have not required them to take charge in resolving conflict and hostilities need to concentrate on being more assertive in conflict situations through understanding, acceptance, and decisive actions.

A Manager Is a Politician

Again, because of limited resources in an organization and because of individual differences in goals and values, a manager must be adept at persuading and compromising in order to promote personal, departmental, and organizational goals. Every effective manager "plays politics" by developing networks of mutual obligations with other managers in the organization. At times this also includes building alliances and coalitions that can be drawn on to win support for critical proposals, decisions, or activities. In order to develop the necessary rapport and to make contacts, female managers are often required to become involved in leisure activities traditionally engaged in by men, like golfing and spectator sports such as baseball and football.

A Manager Is a Diplomat

A manager is the official representative of a working unit in the organization. When attending organizational meetings or dealing with clients, customers, or governmental officials, managers are considered as representatives of the entire organization and of their units in particular. This has important image implications for both the manager and the organization.

A Manager Makes Difficult Decisions

Since no organization runs smoothly at all times, there is no limit to the numbers and types of problems that may occur. Managers are the ones who are expected to come up with the solutions to difficult problems and to follow through on decisions even when such actions may be unpopular. Examples of these are situations in which it is necessary to terminate an employee or make unpopular work assignments. In situations like these personal feelings should be put aside in deference to overall organizational effectiveness.

The summary given above does not begin to exhaust the list of roles that a manager must fill. What it does, however, is to emphasize that managers need to "change hats" frequently and to be aware of what particular role is fitting at a given time. The ability to recognize and switch into appropriate roles is a mark of an effective manager.

FUNCTIONS OF MANAGEMENT

Regardless of the type of organization—educational, business, governmental, military, or social—there are basic managerial functions, or processes, that must be carried out. **Management** is the process of *planning*, *organizing*, *staffing*, *leading*, and *controlling* the efforts of organizational members and using organizational resources to achieve stated organizational objectives. Whether a manager supervises three people or dozens of subordinates, he or she will perform these functions at one time or another.

Planning

Planning is the process of determining goals and how they are to be achieved. No matter how laudable a goal may be, nothing usually happens until a plan of action is developed to achieve it. New Year's resolutions are common examples of unmet goals due to a lack of planning. A plan provides the design for specific courses of action to assure that the necessary things are done to accomplish the goal.

Women as Planners. The traditional female "doer" jobs are confined to specific daily tasks and procedures where women carry out plans of others rather than formulate their own. For many new women managers, therefore, planning is a new dimension of the job. This is also due, in part, to the "helpmate" role mentioned earlier, where women act in submissive, supportive ways, as assistants to men. These roles result in a detachment from goal setting and planning.

When given the opportunities and experience, however, women are just as good at organizational planning as men. Studies by Reif, Newstrom, and Monczka have demonstrated that women's potential for planning is identical to men's based on skill levels in abstract reasoning, analytical thinking, achievement motivation, and adaptability.[2] Countless women have proved this point more pragmatically in mainstream planning ventures in the areas of politics, philanthropy, religious work, and in other service-related organizations.

Planning Aids. To be successful, a plan must have the *support* of upper management as well as those subordinates who will implement it. Plans must be compatible with other current objectives in regard to timeliness and impact. They also must be clearly understood by subordinates and flexible enough to undergo necessary modifications and revisions. To ensure the above, it is helpful to follow McGregor's supportive approach to planning where commitment is sought from all affected through mutual involvement in the determination of both objectives and plans.[3]

The essential steps in formulating a plan have been summarized by Stewart.[4] The prerequisite to planning is *clarity of objectives.* The goal may already be officially expressed, or it may have to be established anew. In either case, the manager might codify the goal in a clear, written statement and communicate it to all concerned. Next, the manager *gathers all pertinent data* and *analyzes* them to *establish reasonable premises* in order to generate realistic *alternative plans.* After the most promising plan has been *decided*, the manager puts it into action by determining its timing, specific activities and responsibilities, and control points. Finally, the manager *communicates* the plan to all subordinates, peers, and supervisors who may be affected so as to *determine who will be responsible* for what, where, and when.

Evaluation of Planning Effectiveness. There are two main tests that determine the effectiveness of a plan:

1. Determine the extent to which it facilitates the *attainment of the objectives.*

2. Determine the extent to which the *gains* attributable to the plan *outweigh* the associated *costs* (e.g., time, money, effort) spent on preparing and executing it.

Checkpoints to be considered when evaluating a plan's chances of meeting the above criteria include: compatibility with other current goals, accessibility of resources required, extent of involvement of all concerned, and degree of acceptance by other managers and subordinates who must implement it. If the plan meets these criteria, it is time to organize resources and schedule the activities necessary to make it work.

Organizing

Plans must be translated into action by establishing priorities, assigning responsibilities, and developing time schedules. The necessary human and material resources must be assembled. Tasks must be defined for individuals and groups, and the authority relationships between them established. Thus, the organizing function starts with, and builds upon, the results of previous planning to develop an organization structure. Through the resulting structure the manager hopes to accomplish the goals determined in the planning stage. **Organizing** is deciding who is going to do what, and how people and activities will be related.

The importance of the organizing function can be seen clearly in a simple story from "Sesame Street," a children's educational television program described by Bracy, Sanford, and Quick, in a book on basic management.[5] The story begins when the King decides that he and all of his subjects will have a picnic. The King calls his subjects together, announces the picnic, and tells them to bring watermelon, potato salad, etc. The subjects leave to prepare the food. On returning to the picnic, it is discovered that everybody brought potato salad and nothing else. Needless to say, the King expresses his disappointment at having no watermelon. Lo and behold, everyone takes the potato salad home and returns with watermelon! Finally, someone suggests that the subjects divide the task up and assign different things for different people to bring. The story closes with a successful picnic.

While the story is simple (and may even be foolish to some), it illustrates the importance of organizing—of dividing up the total work to be done, defining everyone's duties and responsibilities, and delegating the authority necessary to perform the duties and responsibilities.

Organizing is a tool for making order possible in the performance of activities—it makes possible cooperation and coordination. Without organizing, chaos is likely to occur because no one knows who is doing what or who is responsible for what. More specifically, without organizing there is no effective way to prevent duplication of activities, nor is there any means of assuring that all necessary activities are performed.

Organizing results in a task system tied together by authority relationships. This takes place through the process of **delegation** where (1) *responsibility* for duties and tasks is assigned, and (2) *authority* to perform the duties and tasks is granted. The amount of authority delegated depends upon situational factors such as the nature of the tasks, the level of subordinate ability, the results expected, and the need for coordination.

Women as Organizers. In *The Managerial Woman*, Hennig and Jardim summarize that, because women tend to overspecialize in one particular area or task and become "the experts," they develop a block against delegating to less skilled subordinates.[6] Previously held "helpmate-type" jobs may also have provided little in the way of responsibilities requiring delegation. On the other hand, new women managers sometimes are so eager to prove their ability that their quest to show results and earn their wings gets in the way. President Dwight D. Eisenhower coined a slogan which shows the folly of this approach: "There's no telling how much one can accomplish so long as one doesn't need to get all the credit for it."

The above quote demonstrates the main advantage of delegating responsibilities—it allows the manager to "multiply herself," that is, to accomplish many more activities by getting results through other people. It also frees her to do the things only she can accomplish. Finally, it helps develop subordinates. When she delegates, she makes better use of her human resources, develops supervisory depth when she is away, and paves the way for even greater recognition in the long run.

Organizing Aids. After overcoming any unwillingness to let go of things that others can do for the manager, there are several things that she can do to make sure that delegation is effective. These are:

1. Make sure that the objectives, timing, and processes are clear.

2. Indicate the standards and control points by which the work will be judged.

3. Assure the subordinate that the manager is available when needed for necessary advice.

4. Make sure that the subordinate is qualified to handle the task.

5. Build in the necessary authority and announce it to all people involved.

The above guidelines will aid the manager in effective task accomplishment, but they don't free her of her supervisory responsibilities. She still must motivate the subordinates involved and follow through during the process so that mistakes can be intercepted and corrected. These are the tasks of the management functions of leading and controlling. It is easier to lead and control qualified and committed subordinates, however. This type of subordinate can be obtained through the staffing function.

Staffing

Because people are the most critical resource in any organization, the selection, training, and development of employees are among the most critical managerial tasks. **Staffing** is the managerial function which deals with recruiting, placing, training, and developing organizational members.

The Staffing Process. Because most organizations experience a constant turnover of personnel over time, the staffing process is best conceptualized as a series of steps that are performed on a continuing basis to ensure that the organization has the best qualified people in the right positions at all times. The eight major steps in the staffing process, outlined by French in *The Personnel Management Process*, are briefly described below.[7]

1. *Human resource planning*. This step is undertaken to ensure that the current and future personnel needs of the organization are met. It includes the analysis of expected skills needed, predicted vacancies, and projected expansions or reductions as compared to the labor market demographics.

2. *Recruitment*. This is the process of attracting candidates for current or projected job openings. Candidates are located through such sources as advertisements (in newspapers, professional journals, radio, or college campus placement offices), employment agencies, current employees, etc.

3. *Selection*. This is the process of evaluating and choosing from among job applicants. Aids in selection include resumes, interviews, tests, application forms, and reference checks.

4. *Orientation*. This step is undertaken to help the recruit adjust and fit into the organization. Orientation activities include introducing the new employee to current employees, and attending lunches, briefings, and meetings.

5. *Training*. This step is undertaken to help individual employees increase their skills and contributions to the

organization. It may be for the purpose of improving their performance in their current jobs or preparing them for promotions and additional responsibilities.

6. *Performance appraisal.* This process compares the individual employee's actual performance with established criteria and standards. Feedback can then be provided to correct deviations or to reward behavior that is acceptable.

7. *Transfer.* This process shifts personnel among jobs in the organization. **Vertical transfers** are promotions or demotions. **Lateral transfers** are from one position to another at the same level or to a different location.

8. *Separation.* This process involves resignations, layoffs, discharges, or retirements. Retirements may be anticipated through earlier human resource planning, but the study of other types of separations can provide insights into the effectiveness of such matters as the pay scale, management style, selection, and training.

Women and Staffing. Fifteen percent of the women in the work force today hold management jobs, which is more than double the proportion twenty years ago.[8] A number of good reasons are behind this shift. First, there has been substantial government pressure enforcing equal opportunity for women through laws such as the Equal Pay Act and Title VII of the Civil Rights Act. Decisions in court cases have supported these acts and enforced regulations against such illegal practices as discrimination based on sex. Organizations concerned with their public image have hired and promoted more women managers to avoid negative publicity from such organizations as the National Organization for Women (NOW) which could eventually damage the sales of their products to female-dominated markets.

Second, significant demographic changes, such as the dramatic increases in women's educational levels, have produced more and better qualified women in the work force. For example, approximately one half of today's business school graduates at both the undergraduate level and graduate level are women.

Third, the rising cost of living has increased the number of women seeking managerial positions which not only pay more than traditional female-occupied positions, but also allow for substantially better self-satisfaction and personal development.

Finally, human resource planners, many of whom are women, are coming to realize that, to recruit the most capable managerial talent, they must look to the creative resources in the female work force. Overcoming past practices of placing women in "traditional female" positions is still being slowed by many who accept the cultural barriers imposed by the current male-dominated management of most organizations. To counter these practices, many business and government organizations, such as the State of California, have developed training programs to reeducate both male and female managers.[9]

Leading

Leading is the function that links the manager's planned objectives and the achievement of those objectives. As pointed out by Bracy, Sanford, and Quick, the planning, organizing, and staffing functions are preparation for achievement. Through the leadership function, the action needed to actually reach objectives is started and maintained.[10]

Leadership involves *communicating* the what and how of job assignments to subordinates and *motivating* them to do the things necessary to achieve organizational objectives. It is the most *interpersonal* function of management. These components of leadership are so important that a separate chapter on motivation and communication (Chapter 6) is devoted to them.

Looking at well-known examples of effective female leaders, such as Queen Elizabeth I, Florence Nightingale, Indira Gandhi, and Gloria Steinem, demonstrates that a great variety of personalities and styles can be equally effective. Leadership is not a matter of who the person is, but *how* that person influences others. It is situational, and different jobs require different clusters of leadership behaviors. Leadership is also the cultivation of an appropriate organizational climate in which people can grow as they contribute to the organization's objectives. Through a combination of technical, human, and conceptual skills, the effective leader is able to persuade others to work enthusiastically and competently toward defined organizational objectives.

__Women as Leaders.__ The above examples of female leaders indicate that women are able to rise to prominent leadership positions. The vast majority of organizational leaders today, however, are men. Women usually occupy lower status, lower influence jobs. What keeps more women from moving into leadership positions?

Some of the answers are evident in commonly accepted myths and stereotypes. One traditional stereotype is that men have innately superior leadership skills. In leadership situations Hollander has pointed out that male success is usually attributed to skill and ability.[11] When women are successful as leaders, on the other hand, it is usually attributed to luck, or whom they know. Since organizations support leaders who have skills and ability rather those who are just lucky, women are unable to move into leadership positions.

There is also a prevalent view that women make poor managers. McGregor has written that the model of a successful manager in American society is based entirely on masculine traits like competitiveness, aggressiveness, and firmness.[12] The model does not include feminine traits like softness, dependency, or emotionality. Although this stereotype is gradually shifting, it continues to contribute to beliefs that men can't be effective when working for women and that women's family roles interfere with their work responsibilities.

Another problem is the fact that currently there is such a small number of visible women leaders to serve as appropriate female role models. New female managers have few examples to identify with and to emulate.

__Leadership Aids.__ Although there are no "universal" characteristics of effective leaders, there are valuable assets that a manager can develop more fully to enhance her leadership effectiveness. Some of those pointed out by the American Management Association are summarized below:[13]

1. **Performance**, or the ability to carry out current duties exceptionally well. Competence in doing one's job generates respect from subordinates and motivates them to be effective also in their jobs.

2. **Initiative**, or the ability to be a "self-starter." Subordinates

look to their managers to point them in the right direction and to provide the structure in which they can perform their own activities.

3. **Acceptance**, or the ability to gain respect and win the confidence of others. One of the keys to being accepted by others is to treat them with respect and to listen carefully when they try to express their own needs and concerns.

4. **Good judgment**, or the ability to reach sound conclusions based on all of the evidence available in a situation where a decision has to be made.

5. **Communication**, or the ability to "get through" to people at all levels. Chapter 6 deals with essential communication skills and strategies for a manager.

6. **Accomplishment**, or the amount and quality of work produced mainly through the effective use of one's own time. Time management also will be discussed in more detail in Chapter 5.

7. **Flexibility**, or the ability to cope with change and to adjust to the unexpected. In working with different personalities and different situations, it is extremely important to be able to see things from different points of view and to adapt one's own interpersonal style to meet the needs of changing situations.

8. **Objectivity**, or the ability to control personal feelings in an open-minded manner. In dealing with a group of subordinates, it is extremely important not to appear biased. The manager must show that she has considered all the relevant facts involved in making objective decisions, especially when the results affect those working for her.

Task and Relationship Behaviors. In order for work groups to operate effectively, two major aspects of the leadership function must be exhibited. The first is the **task-related** (or problem-solving) **behavior** which is aimed at accomplishing the objectives of the group itself. The second is the **relationship-related behavior** which involves group maintenance. This includes anything which helps the group to operate more smoothly and to feel good about the other members within the group.

At times it is more important to show a task-related behavior, such as forcefully encouraging the group to make an important decision or to get on with the job. At other times the relationship-related behavior is more important as, for example, when it is necessary to mediate group disagreements. An individual who is able to perform both roles successfully is in a much better position to be an effective leader.

The degree of effectiveness that a leader exhibits is most appropriately measured by the accomplishments of her followers. This in turn depends on how much the followers understand about the goals they are pursuing, how they perform, how unified they are in their work setting, and how committed they are toward the attainment of organizational goals. The effective leader, therefore, determines the most appropriate and productive behavior for herself in dealing with her followers, depending on her relevant goals, environment, and leadership abilities. She also integrates the organizational values, group values, and individual values effectively in order to attain the company goals over the long term.

In addition to giving subordinates legitimate directions, the leader, by definition, must be able to influence followers to carry out directions effectively. A manager, for example, may direct a subordinate to perform a certain task; but it is her *continuous* influence over that subordinate which will determine if the task is carried out properly. The control system she establishes and the way she uses it are key components in making sure that the expected results are achieved.

Controlling

Controlling involves monitoring what is actually happening and correcting deviations from plans. The best attempts at planning, organizing, staffing, and leading do not always produce the anticipated results. Controlling is the function that makes sure the other management functions pay off. It also serves as the link to future planning, organizing, staffing, and leading.

There are three basic elements in the control process: (1) establishing valid, current standards of performance; (2) measuring actual performance against established performance standards, and (3) using the feedback process in taking corrective measures to improve situations. Unless there are standards against which performance can be measured, control is impossible. Specific standards can be developed from the performance goals themselves. Examples of standards are units of output produced, the time taken to accomplish certain activities, or any other factor indicating goal achievement.

Once the appropriate standards and measuring scales have been developed, the actual measurement of results can be made. This includes the collection of data and comparing them to the control standards. Conclusions can then be reached regarding performance effectiveness. If deviations from established standards are found, the manager must first identify and analyze the real cause of the deviation. The results may be positive or negative. A positive performance should be complimented with sincere praise or financial rewards. If the result is negative, the manager must plan and initiate corrective action.

Women as Controllers. The primary barrier to effective controlling is that many people see it as a negative and unpleasant function. Most people don't enjoy being thought of as the person who checks up on others by constantly looking over their shoulders. Also, disciplining and reprimanding subordinates whose behavior is found to deviate from accepted standards is not a pleasant task. For some new woman managers these actions may be out of character. Thus, controlling may present internal as well as interpersonal conflicts for them.

New woman managers should bear in mind that the purpose of control is positive in that it facilitates the accomplishment of organizational objectives. As a result, it benefits all involved in many direct and indirect ways. Also, many of the negatively viewed aspects of controlling can be made more palatable by dealing with them in a positive, problem-solving way. Chapter 9 presents some guidelines in dealing with problem employees.

Controlling Aids. There are many control techniques which can aid in implementing the controlling process. The most useful are _budgets, work standards,_ and _time schedules._ Other techniques include _direct observations, progress reports,_ and _formal performance evaluations._ If corrective action is warranted, it can be positively taken through activities like *interviewing, counseling,* and *joint problem solving.* The following criteria can be used to evaluate the effectiveness of any control system:

1. *Is the system economical?* It makes no sense to invest more resources in the control process than the activity itself might save. It is important to include time as a resource in this cost/benefit calculation.

2. *Is it efficient?* The best time to learn of deviations, particularly negative ones, is before they occur. Since this is seldom possible when dealing with people, the next best thing is to make sure negative deviations are reported in time to make appropriate corrections.

3. *Is it understandable?* Clear, unambiguous feedback is just as important to subordinates as it is to managers. Managers must clearly understand what went wrong and why. Subordinates must clearly understand what needs to be done when taking corrective actions.

4. *Is it acceptable?* People who use and are affected by controls must believe that they are fair and useful. An acceptable control system provides the basic motivation to use controls properly. A fundamental prerequisite to acceptance involves an *understanding of the system, how it works,* and *why it is necessary.*

VARIATIONS OF THE MANAGERIAL PROCESSES

Every manager must plan, organize, staff, lead, and control, but different managers may go about these activities in different ways. The manager of a small antique shop may plan quite a bit less formally than an engineering department manager charged with designing and supplying small mechanical parts to large aerospace companies. A manager in a newly formed company may find that more time is required in coordinating work since a new organization requires the right sequencing of activities of many different and independent groups. Every manager will have different problems and ways of leading. If a manager has workers who are engaged in routine and boring work, different styles of motivation are required for those workers than the styles appropriate for people working in fast-paced occupations with a lot of excitement and challenge.

The emphasis on the different managerial processes also varies depending on the manager's position in the organizational hierarchy. Upper level executives spend more time planning, while lower level supervisors spend more time controlling. The types of decisions made at the top levels have broader perspectives and longer time horizons than those made at the lower levels which are more specific and sometimes more urgent. All managers must manage, but the appropriate techniques vary according to management level.

The previous descriptions of planning, organizing, staffing, leading and controlling evoke images of management as rational, systematic, and reflective. However, several researchers who have spent a considerable amount of time observing managers in action agree that, in reality, management is more chaotic than systematic, and more emotional than rational. The manager's day is fractured into an astonishingly large number of contacts with different people and different problems. Henry Mintzberg systematically studied managers on a daily basis and reported what they actually do in his book, *The Nature of Managerial Work*. In general, Mintzberg found that managers can expect no concentration of efforts; rather, managers' activities are characterized by brevity, fragmentation, and variety. There is no break in the pace of activity from the time a manager arrives in the morning until he or she leaves in the evening. On an average day, managers open 36 pieces of mail, make 5 phone calls, and attend 8 meetings. A true break seldom occurs. The best most managers can hope for is coffee during meetings and lunch during formal business meetings.[14]

Just what managers are doing in this whirlwind of activity was the subject for another group of researchers. They questioned 452 managers from 11 management levels in companies that ranged in size from 100 to more than 4,000 employees. They were asked about how much of the workday they spent on 8 different activities. The results are listed in Table 2-1.

TABLE 2-1

PERCENTAGE OF WORKDAY SPENT BY MANAGER ON EIGHT ACTIVITIES

Activities	Percentage
Supervising	28.4
Planning	19.5
Coordinating	15.0
Evaluating	12.7
Investigating	12.6
Negotiating	6.0
Staffing	4.1
Representing	1.7
TOTAL	100.0%

Source: T. A. Mahoney, T. H. Jerdee, and J. J. Carroll, "The Jobs of Management," *Industrial Relations,* (February 1965), pp. 97-110. Reproduced with permission.

Given this information, it is evident that although planning, organizing, staffing, leading, and controlling are necessary, most managers find themselves attempting these activities under conditions of brevity and fragmentation. The nature of managerial work is extremely fast paced. A manager has to deal with constant interruptions, deal with many problems simultaneously, and juggle priorities for action. Constant awareness and application of the management functions can help keep a manager in charge of turbulent environments. Appropriate adaptation of these functions to fit particular situations can also help the manager progress up the organizational ladder.

The remaining chapters will provide some fundamental strategies and skills that can enhance the woman manager's career. These strategies are drawn from our experiences as consultants to large and small organizations, from our university teaching experiences, and from counseling many successful women managers. We surveyed 246 women holding mid- to upper level management positions to learn what they viewed as the most favorable guidelines for women in management. Their insights are dispersed throughout this book in the form of quotes, comments, and case examples. We hope that they will provide valuable ideas and inspiration to help the woman manager in her career.

ACTION GUIDELINES

Being accepted into the managerial ranks is only the *first step*. New managers need to demonstrate their competence in performing management functions and their ability to fit into the social milieu if they are going to stay there and continue to advance in their careers. Both seasoned male and female managers will be carefully watching the female newcomer's performance to see how well she learns and adapts. Several guidelines can be drawn to facilitate women's success in overcoming traditional barriers and developing managerial skills.

1. *Avoid traditional female roles.* New women managers may be tempted to yield to the pressures of male majorities and conform to their expectations of passive, dependent, or "helpmate" types of roles. It would be easier for everyone if tradition were confirmed. Being new in a management position, however, provides the opportunity to grow and to demonstrate creativity, assertiveness, decisiveness, and ability to take on responsibilities independently. Although holding out may be tough at first, continued demonstration of managerial competence may cause these and other pressures to subside and facilitate acceptance as a peer.

2. *Clarify your managerial role expectations.* In general, managers are responsible for making efficient and effective use of the organization's resources to accomplish the organization's goals. It is important to clarify how this is expected to be done in any manager's particular situation. The new woman manager should find out by asking questions and talking to other managers about their experiences and techniques. She should find out what are the unwritten responsibilities to be accounted for, and ask such questions as: How are conflicts expected to be resolved? What managerial styles seem most effective? What alliances and coalitions exist, and how can they be used to facilitate the manager's job?

3. *Become proficient in the functions of management*. Successful managers take the time necessary to adequately develop a plan for accomplishing objectives assigned to them. A few minutes of planning and organizing one's time and resources at the beginning of each day can save hours of confusion and anxiety for both the manager and those working for her. The same is true in even greater magnitude for long-term projects.

Finally, in order to assure goal implementation and accomplishment, the manager should do everything possible to build the understanding, commitment, and support she needs among those affected by her plans. It will also make the jobs of leading and controlling much easier because her subordinates will already understand and accept what they are doing as important and legitimate.

FOOTNOTES

1. J. A. F. Stoner, *Management* (2d ed.; Englewood Cliffs, NJ: Prentice-Hall, 1978), pp. 11-13.

2. W. Reif, J. Newstrom, and R. Monczka, "Exploding Some Myths About Women Managers," *California Management Review* (Summer, 1975), pp. 72-79.

3. D. McGregor, "An Uneasy Look at Performance Appraisal," *Harvard Business Review*, Vol. 35, No. 3 (May-June, 1975), pp. 89-94.

4. N. Stewart, *The Effective Woman Manager* (New York: John Wiley & Sons, 1978), pp. 34-35.

5. Hyler J. Bracy, Aubrey Sanford, and J. C. Quick, *Basic Management: An Experience Based Approach* (Rev. ed.; Dallas: Business Publications Inc., 1981), p. 126.

6. Margaret Hennig and Anne Jardim, *The Managerial Woman* (New York: Pocket Books, 1978), pp. 59-60.

7. W. French, *The Personnel Management Process* (4th ed.; Boston: Houghton Mifflin Company, 1978).

8. A. L. McLabre, Jr., "Women at Work: As Their Ranks Swell, Women

Holding Jobs Reshape U.S. Society," *The Wall Street Journal*, August 28, 1978, p. 1.

9. K. Anundsen, "Keys to Developing Managerial Women," *Management Review* (February, 1979), pp. 55-58.

10. Bracy, Sanford, and Quick, *op. cit.*

11. E. P. Hollander, "Composition Counts: The Behavior of Women and Men in Groups," (From a symposium on Women, Gender, and Social Psychology, presented at the Eastern Psychological Association Convention, Philadelphia, April, 1979).

12. D. McGregor, *The Professional Manager* (New York: McGraw Hill, 1967), p. 23.

13. Stewart, *op.cit.*, pp. 8-9.

14. Henry Mintzberg, *The Nature of Managerial Work* (New York: Harper & Row, 1973), p. 30.

CHAPTER 3

Projecting Your Image

__OUTLINE__

I.   First Impressions Based on Appearance

      A.   Decisions Made by Others
      B.   Case Examples
      C.   Specific Guidelines on Clothing
      D.   Guidelines on the Use of Accessories
      E.   Summary

II.   Depth of Knowledge

III.   Breadth of Knowledge

IV.   Versatility

V.   Enthusiasm

VI.   Sincerity

Action Guidelines

Image is a term used to describe the picture a person projects to other people. A person's positive image can set the stage for success in business, while a negative image may set the stage for failure. In many respects the image a person projects is very much like a picture puzzle. The total image one projects to others is made up of several components. Among these are: (1) the first impressions based on appearance, (2) depth of knowledge, (3) breadth of knowledge, (4) versatility, (5) enthusiasm, and (6) sincerity. This chapter deals with these six areas which we consider to be the critical components of one's image.

FIRST IMPRESSIONS BASED ON APPEARANCE

For the businesswoman in the 1980s, there is a move toward a working uniform. In the corporate world the suit is the quickest signal of executive status. How do managers distinguish the female secretary from the female executive? *Dress is the easiest way to tell them apart.* The executive should *look* like an executive. Dressing in the corporate uniform is the first step. A 48-year-old female Director of Personnel responded to our survey as follows:

> I personally have experimented with the "dress" issue. I found that when I dress conservatively, and especially in black, I immediately am treated with more authority, power, and respect than when I wear "trendy" or fashionable clothes. I believe that the conservative approach is more comfortable to executives—you somehow become more identifiable and are not "different" from them! "Differentness" seems to be a threat when you are female and they are male!

If a woman manager is going to command the respect and authority necessary to accomplish her objectives, *it is necessary for her to look like a manager and come across with an image that matches the expectations of those who are working for her and with her.* As irrational as it may seem, *people do judge a book by its cover.* It is important for a new female manager to present positive first impressions so that others will continue to have an open mind and discover her genuine talents and skills.

Managers who look and act like executives do have a decided edge over those who do not convey the appropriate image. This is particularly important for new women managers. Positive first impressions are lasting impressions and can provide a continuing effect for enhancing effectiveness. Negative initial impressions can cut off any chance of later being perceived as a competent manager. This tendency to preserve initial impressions is called **primacy effect** by social psychologists. According to Rubin, the general principle is that first impressions establish the mental framework in which a person is received, and later evidence is either ignored or reinterpreted to coincide with the framework.[1]

Discrimination on the basis of appearance is a *fact of life* in the business world.[2] The image a woman manager projects *can even be as important to job success as her skills*. Her ability to get a job and advance to a position of greater responsibility will often depend on the impression she makes on others. According to Carr-Ruffino, the people selected for higher level positions tend to look and act as if they fit the new role even *before* they're given the nod.[3] The following discussion provides suggestions which can aid in establishing a positive *and lasting first impression* as an effective manager.

Decisions Made by Others

Clothing is a powerful medium for projecting one's image. Clothing acts as a cue to those around a person. It helps strangers to identify that person and reinforces the image held by that person's acquaintances, friends, and business associates. What a female manager wears *immediately establishes her credibility and likability*.[4] When she steps into a room, even though no one in that room knows her or has seen her before, they will make at least ten decisions about her based solely on her appearance.[5] They may make many more, but she can be assured that they will make decisions about her:

1. Economic level

2. Educational level

3. Trustworthiness

4. Social position

5. Level of sophistication

6. Economic heritage

7. Social heritage

8. Educational heritage

9. Success

10. Moral character

It is important that a female manager make a favorable first impression so that the decisions made about her will also be favorable. Knowing how to use clothing to establish herself in whatever role she wants to play can help her win that role more quickly.

Case Examples

There are many women who are not sure of what role they want to play. There are others who intentionally dress in a less professional manner and send out the wrong message, afraid that dressing well might detract from their intellectual profile. One senior partner in a law firm told us about a young woman who had entered the firm with high grades from law school and who seemed to have a brilliant future ahead of her. The only problem was that no one in the firm wanted to introduce her to clients. "We were desperate," he said. "We wanted to retain her but she dressed so badly. We couldn't let any of our clients meet her." Fortunately for this young woman, some very good friends took her aside and taught her the rules of dress. Her appearance improved, and later the senior partner remarked, "She's now on her way to becoming a partner herself."

A woman's clothing immediately establishes her in a social order whether or not she is aware of it. One of our brightest MBA students interviewed for a banking position. She was told that her record was excellent but that she obviously did not want a job in that field. Shocked, she went home and looked at herself in the mirror. Only then did she realize the kind of message she was sending out. She had dressed for the interview in the type of outfit she typically wore as a student: a full, printed dirndl skirt and a soft peasant blouse. The interviewer at the bank had suggested she might be more at home in journalism or the arts. In fact, she hadn't really wanted a job in banking and now holds a very responsible position with a graphic arts firm. She had revealed herself through her clothes without even knowing how much she was telling about herself.

If a woman knows what position she wants in a company, she can use clothing to help her get the job. The female secretary who wants to become a manager will get there faster if she starts dressing like the women managers in that company. The woman who wants to be chairperson of a group will have a better chance if she looks like a leader. A 28-year-old woman working her way up in the corporate ranks in the hotel industry vowed never again to wear pants to work. In her words:

> When you're trying to get up the corporate ladder, there's a point when everybody has the same background. When you want to be recognized, a lot has to do with the way you project yourself. You have to play the part before you get it.

Specific Guidelines on Clothing

As we stated earlier, the suit is the accepted form of dress for the female executive. In other fields, there are other appropriate signals. In retailing, for instance, the hierarchy is established not only by the price of one's clothes but also the forwardness of their design. For the woman wanting to advance in the managerial ranks, the best advice is to dress like those people whose positions she aspires to. With skillful dressing she can evoke a positive response and enhance her image as a successful manager.

To project authority and success, a woman should dress in a conservative manner in clothing made of natural fibers. This means that she will probably be spending more than she wants and possibly more than she can afford at first, but such clothing will last longer and look much better. Fabrics like wool or cotton for suits, and silk for blouses, should be chosen. The female manager should wear apparel in colors and patterns that are conservative and congruent with each other. She doesn't need a lot of clothes, but the clothes she has should be of very high quality and look like it. Also, she should wear leather shoes.

Other more specific guidelines on appropriate dress that have been developed by Molloy are as follows:[6]

1. Establish personal dress and grooming standards appropriate for the company where you wish to work. Before you apply for a job, try to find out what the workers there are wearing. If in doubt, dress conservatively. If you find out the dress code is more relaxed, you can adjust to it later. When you actually begin work, identify the most successful people in the organization and imitate their manner of dress.

2. Dress for the job you want, not the job you have. If you are currently a secretary and desire to become an executive, don't continue to dress like a secretary. Employees can communicate with their clothing that they are satisfied with their position. Some employers say they can walk into a company office and see who is ready for a promotion.

3. Avoid wearing the newest dress fad in a business setting. In most cases, the world of business is more conservative than the college environment, the arts, or the world of sports. If you are a "fashion setter," you might be viewed as unstable or lacking in sincerity. To be taken seriously, avoid clothing that is too flashy!

4. When you select a wardrobe, be sure to consider regional differences in dress and grooming standards. Geography is a major factor regarding how people should dress. What may be suitable business apparel for a receptionist working in Los Angeles may be too casual in Des Moines. Pay close attention to local customs and traditions when establishing

your personal dress and grooming standards.

These guidelines were supported by several successful women managers who responded to our own survey. A 35-year-old Regional Manager of Employees Communications at Atlantic Richfield Co. put it this way:

> On the subject of clothing ... I feel that women should be flexible in their dress. For myself, if I am attending a meeting with all executives, I will dress conservatively (suit or dress).
>
> However, if I go into the field (I work for an oil company), I will show up in jeans. This does not "ruin" my image. In fact, by dressing to fit the need, I can accomplish my goals better; and the (mostly) men I talk with there are more willing to work with me. If I showed up in a suit and low heels, I think many of them would freeze up around me.
>
> In my job (I am an industrial editor), I must deal with *all* levels of employees and wish to be "approachable" to them (for story ideas). Therefore, I tend to wear fairly casual clothes in everyday situations around my office.
>
> Another comment I have heard a number of times from the men I work with is—*don't* wear perfume in the office. That's a real turnoff!

The quality of a woman's wardrobe will influence the image she projects. The money she spends on career apparel should be viewed as an investment with each item carefully selected to look and fit well. A suit or dress purchased "off the rack" at a discount store may save dollars initially, but can cost her more if it doesn't help her get that promotion she wants. Clothes purchased at bargain prices often wear out quickly. The less money she has, the more important it is for her to buy quality clothing.

Guidelines on the Use of Accessories

Closely related to clothing are *accessories* such as jewelry, handbags, briefcases, and luggage. Any jewelry worn should be the real thing. A watch is a must—and an attractive, good-quality watch can be purchased at a reasonable price. Again, because the woman manager wants to establish a conservative but high-quality image, she should be careful not to overkill even if she can afford it.

Luggage and briefcases make a definite statement. The woman manager's colleagues will note exactly what it is she is claiming at the baggage terminals. Like her clothes and shoes, accessories should look serious and professional. This means no pastels and no flowers, but preferably something made of leather with a conservative design. A good-quality briefcase costing between $150 and $200 will be money well spent. A shocking pink synthetic handbag will kill any possibility a woman might ever have of being taken seriously as a manager. Also, both her briefcase and handbag should be kept highly organized. Rummaging around in them only makes her look like an "inefficient woman." She should make sure to include a very good pen and pencil set. Men have these and so should women.

Summary

The overall image the woman manager is striving for is the well (but not overly) made-up image: pulled together, manicured and pedicured, fashionable but not faddish, and every single hair in place! Of course, this is an extremely tough image to pull off especially when she is elbow-deep in work and hassled under pressure. Many current books give women detailed advice on image, ranging from the best colors to wear to ways of making the most of their body type.[7]

In short, the woman manager is trying to appear as a person of authority who is serious about her job and the results that she is trying to obtain. This means that she needs to look self-assured and assertive. This look is conservative and expensive. She shouldn't jeopardize it by looking too cute, too pretty, or too frilly—in other words, too feminine. Her clothes, voice, grooming, handshake, and body postures make a significant difference in the reception she receives from other people. First impressions do count! And if she does not present an appropriate image to create a positive impression on other people, that poor image will count against her. She should do the best she can to make it count for her.

DEPTH OF KNOWLEDGE

Depth of knowledge refers to how well a person knows his or her subject—or particular area of expertise. For a woman this is extremely important because people are watching her. For example, if she is a marketing manager, does she know what there is to know about the products she is responsible for, as well as the markets for them? If she is a personnel manager, does she know her personnel and is she thoroughly familiar with the employment policies and procedures of her organization, as well as with the laws that are applicable to them? Do other employees come to her because they respect her expertise, or do her subordinates, peers, and superiors avoid her because of her shallow knowledge in her particular area of work? Does her depth of knowledge project credibility and command respect from her subordinates, or can she hear them saying the following about her? "I could do her job as well as she can."

In addition, how well does she know her company and industry? Is she up to date on her company's relative strengths and weaknesses compared to the competition? Being an expert in her specific line of work may help her retain her current managerial position, but *also* being an expert about her company and industry's overall status could mark her as a candidate for a higher level position. The woman manager should take advantage of any relevant training programs that her company may offer to improve herself.

A 46-year-old female president of a New York City mail-order marketing company responded to our survey with these additional guidelines:

> Read the relevant business publications or trade papers—they *are* vital. Attending specific seminars and meeting people at trade associations, conventions, etc., are also important. When you increase your depth of knowledge, you will command respect from your employees, peers, and superiors by projecting an image of intelligence and credibility.

BREADTH OF KNOWLEDGE

The ability to converse with others on topics outside of one's particular area of expertise indicates that person's **breadth of**

knowledge. For instance, does the woman manager know what are the latest developments in world events? Is she familiar with the latest books and movies that are popular? Does she know who won the football game on Saturday? In addition, can she converse with people about things that are of interest to *them*?

Many male managers assume that women are interested only in clothes, recipes, children, and looking for a husband. By increasing her breadth of knowledge, the woman manager will be able to develop rapport more easily. By not restricting the topic of conversation to something she alone desires to talk about, she will allow people to be more comfortable in conversing with her. When she is willing and able to talk to them, they will feel much more comfortable being in her presence. In fact, people will go out of their way to be in her presence and talk with her. They will feel that she shares something with them. The more people feel they share things in common, the better they like each other. So, by increasing her breadth of knowledge, the woman manager will increase her circle of influence with various types of people. Even if she is not up to date or knowledgeable about another person's topic of conversation, she should show interest in it by asking questions. This is one of the best ways to learn.

The responsibility for increasing one's breadth of knowledge falls totally *on one's shoulders*. There are a number of things that the woman manager can do today, regardless of her age or background, to increase her breadth of knowledge. She should read a local newspaper every day. If possible, she should read it from cover to cover. In addition to the daily newspaper, she might read one of the major news magazines weekly. This will give her a good background in national and international events as well as some additional knowledge in the areas of education, the arts, sports, books, movies, etc. She should make an effort to read at least two books per year outside her normal area of interest, and try to mix fiction and nonfiction.

Finally, the woman manager should make optimum use of typical nonproductive time spent on such activities as bathing, putting on makeup, driving to and from work, cooking, cleaning, and anything else she can think of. She can make use of this nonproductive time by watching a morning or evening television news show, listening to radio news programs anytime throughout the day, and listening to audio cassettes of books and/or educational materials. She should remember that increasing her breadth of knowledge comes most easily from reading, listening, and interacting with other people.

VERSATILITY

Versatility refers to one's willingness and skill in adapting his or her behavior to best relate to other people. Very simply, it is good manners. It is where one steps out of his or her own "comfort zone" in order to communicate and interact effectively with other persons on their level.

Versatility is something one does to oneself, not to others. A woman manager practices versatility every time she slows down to interact with another person who does not feel comfortable moving as fast as she does. She is practicing versatility when she takes time to listen to another individual's personal story rather than getting right down to the task at hand. She is practicing versatility when she makes an effort to speak on the same level as the other person. She is practicing versatility when she covers a topic in much more detail than is typical of her style. She is practicing versatility when she is simply making an effort to meet the personal and professional needs of other people and make them feel comfortable.

Versatility is required because of the fact that people are different and like to be treated differently. When the manager treats all people the same or treats them inappropriately, they feel uncomfortable with her and the tension level rises. This has an adverse effect on the trust relationship she is trying to establish with others.

ENTHUSIASM

Who's your favorite entertainer? Pretend that you are going to a benefit concert tonight to see your favorite entertainer whom we'll call Tammy Linn. The tickets cost $25 per person. An entertainer typically sings 12 to 15 songs during the course of a concert. As Tammy Linn comes on stage, the house thunders with applause. Then she walks up to the microphone and starts singing. She sings 15 songs as well as you have ever heard her sing them. But she sings them in succession, with no attempt to build rapport with the audience. At the end of the 15th song, Tammy thanks the audience for coming to see her and walks off the stage. How well do you think you and your date would have enjoyed that concert?

If you are like most people, you would feel like you were cheated because the entertainer did not talk with the audience, did not build rapport, and did not show any enthusiasm at all. Even though Tammy sang those 15 songs as well as you have ever heard them sung by anybody, you would still feel cheated. Would it improve your opinion of her if you knew that she didn't feel very well because she stayed out late the night before and had a hangover at the time of the concert? Would it improve your attitude any if you knew that, just prior to coming out on stage, she had an argument with her business manager about an advertising contract? Again, if you are like most people, these revelations would not in any way change your feeling that you had been cheated by the concert. If Tammy Linn had just shown a bit more enthusiasm and warmth to the audience, you would probably feel much differently. You might even feel enthused or elated.

When you show lack of enthusiasm for your job or your company, do you think your peers really know or even care why you are not acting enthused? Shouldn't they have the same feelings toward you as you had toward Tammy Linn? Wouldn't they feel cheated by a manager who lacked enthusiasm, much as you would feel cheated by an entertainer who lacked enthusiasm?

Most managers like to see enthusiasm in their employees. Enthusiastic employees seem to work better than those who are not enthused. If a manager wants her employees to have enthusiasm, she must project enthusiasm herself! It doesn't just happen. Enthusiasm is like a contagious disease—it's catching. When the manager outwardly shows enthusiasm about herself, her job, and her company, the same attitude will rub off on her employees. They will be enthused.

SINCERITY

Being sincere means being genuine and not faking it. The manager should make a concerted and genuine effort if she is going to change her image with respect to the critical components we have discussed in this chapter. As with any change of behavior, when the manager initially tries it, it will feel a little bit uncomfortable to her. But if she does it long enough and is sincere about it, it will become a part of her. This sincerity, or lack thereof, will be projected to other people and does become part of the total image she projects to others. If she comes across as insincere to other people, it will have a more damaging effect on her relationships with them than if she had violated all the other components of her image. So, above all else, the manager should be sincere in her interactions with other people and project that sincerity to them.

ACTION GUIDELINES

The image a manager projects to others will help to maximize or minimize her interpersonal success. The response she receives from the world around her is a measure of her success in interpersonal relations. From the beginning to the end of every transaction with another person, she is on stage. Every word, gesture, expression, and impression that she projects will be seen and evaluated, consciously or subconsciously, by that other person. Therefore, she should go through great pains to make sure that the image she projects to other people, in each and every transaction, is an image that helps facilitate communication and build productive relationships.

FOOTNOTES

1. Zick Rubin, "The Rise and Fall of First Impressions—How People Are Perceived," in B. Patton and K. Tiffen, II, (eds.), *Interpersonal Communication in Action* (New York: Harper & Row, 1977), p. 150.

2. Egon Von Ferstenberg, *The Power Look* (New York: Holt-Rinehart-Winston, 1978).

3. Norma Carr-Ruffino, *The Promotable Woman* (Belmont, CA: Wadsworth Publishing Co., 1985), p. 85.

4. John T. Molloy, *The Woman's Dress for Success Book* (New York: Warner Books, 1977).

5. William Thourlby, *You Are What You Wear—The Key to Business Success* (Kansas City: Sheed Andrews and McMeel, 1978), p. 1.

6. Molloy, *op. cit.*

7. C. Jackson, *Color Me Beautiful* (New York: Ballantine Books, 1980). See also B. August, *The Complete Bonnie August Dress Thin System* (New York: Rawson, Wade Publishers, 1984).

CHAPTER 4

Finding Mentors

OUTLINE

I.   What Is a Mentor?

II.   Is a Mentor Really Necessary?

      A.   The Pros
      B.   The Cons
      C.   Research Results

III.   What Can a Mentor Do for You?

      A.   The Mentor's Role as Coach
      B.   The Mentor's Role as Godfather

IV.   How to Find a Mentor

      A.   Make Your Goals Known
      B.   Seek High Visibility and Document Your Accomplishments
      C.   Use the Networking System
      D.   Remain Professional

V.   Problems Encountered in the Mentor Relationship

      A.   Traditional Cultural Conditioning
      B.   Sexual Attraction
      C.   The Servant Trap
      D.   Difficulty in Letting Go

VI.   Can Women Be Mentors?

Action Guidelines

Mentor mania has swept across business organizations today. It is generally agreed that, whether or not a woman in the world of business needs a man, she needs a mentor. Very few female employees make it alone. They need someone to lead the way, to encourage them, and to give them support. When successful women executives talk about their luck or the various forces that helped them get where they are, many of them mention another significant person.

Do you recall what happened in November of 1980? The Mary Cunningham-William Agee relationship at the Bendix Corporation in Detroit made front-page news that month. Twenty-nine-year-old Cunningham, fresh out of Harvard Business School, joined Bendix in June of 1979 as executive assistant to Agee, the company's 43-year-old chairman and chief executive officer. A year later, Agee gave her a bigger title and additional responsibilities as vice-president for corporate and public affairs. Three months after that she was promoted to fill the vacancy of vice-president for strategic planning. Cunningham's rapid rise in the corporation was facilitated by her ability and relationship with Agee.

Agee exposed Cunningham to the Bendix world. She called herself his "alter ego" and "most trusted confidante." He agreed that she was his best friend. Their relationship was one of friendship built on trust. Agee provided valuable information concerning company politics and provided contacts both inside and outside the organization. He used his influence to speed her entry and advancement into top management at the corporation. He acted as teacher, counselor, and guide. He also offered moral support during her difficult emotional times. Agee enhanced Cunningham's skills and intellectual development.[1] In summary, Agee was Cunningham's mentor.

What exactly is a mentor? Is a mentor really necessary? What can a mentor do for the woman manager? How can she find a mentor? What problems can she encounter in the mentor relationship? Can women be mentors? This chapter will attempt to answer all these questions.

WHAT IS A MENTOR?

The dictionary definition of a mentor is a wise and trusted teacher. It originates from Greek mythology. Ever since the poet

Homer's faithful and wise Mentor first advised Odysseus, wise individuals have counseled, taught, coached, and sponsored the young. A commonly accepted definition of a **mentor** is a *senior person who undertakes to guide a younger person's career development*. The mentor acts as a teacher, counselor, and coach to the younger, inexperienced person in the matter of the latter's career, just as Agee acted toward Cunningham. The mentor can be within the protégé's organization or outside of it. The mentor can be a supervisor, company executive, associate, husband, wife, friend, professor, or counselor. The mentor helps open doors for the protégé and helps that person learn to make her or his own decisions through support and feedback. The relationship is based on intellectual and emotional exchange which offers challenges and excitement.

In actuality, the role of a mentor conforms very closely to these definitions. One female manager responding to our survey said of her mentor:

> This is a very political place and my mentor is a very political person. He watches out for me and talks me up to other people. Many of the men I work for find me threatening because I work too hard. They try to lock me out of knowing what's going on around here. It's important to me to have at least as much information as the people who are trying to stab me in the back. My mentor is my key to the men's room.

Other responses to our survey highlighted the same political role played by other mentors. An educational administrator in a business organization said the following about her relationship with her male mentor: "A male mentor is needed in order to obtain a challenging position. The corporation is a male-dominated atmosphere. I was promoted quickly because of my male mentor. I would never have made it without him."

A television production executive stated, "A mentor is a person who opens doors for you and who has such confidence in you that you have confidence in yourself. By the time you're trying to climb the corporate ladder, if you don't have a mentor, others do."

IS A MENTOR REALLY NECESSARY?

Most people seem to think that mentors are necessary, although a few believe otherwise. Below are some reasons for and against the use of mentors, followed by results of recent research on the subject.

The Pros

A mentor may be necessary at two crucial stages of a woman's climb to the upper levels of management. The first period of need occurs during the early phase of a woman's career when she first sees her work as more than just a job and realizes that it may be what she will be doing for the rest of her life. At this early stage of her career development, a personal and parental sort of mentoring is common. This early mentor is a teacher. The protégée not only learns more about the job but is also initiated into game playing, political techniques, image building, and becoming a team member.

The second crucial stage during which a woman needs a mentor comes when it's time for a final push to the top rungs of the ladder. According to Halcomb, the mentor's function at this stage is to provide a "seal of approval."[2] This enables the protégée to gain the respect of others above and below on the ladder of command, as well as that of those outside the organization. For a woman, the endorsement of a male mentor seems essential in the corporate world. Halcomb pointed out in an article titled "The Top Women in Business" that seven of the ten women featured were the daughters, wives, or widows of top executives, while the other three had had mentors who "took them to the top." There seemed to be a necessity for a top man to stand behind a woman saying, in effect, "She's okay. She can do it. She belongs."

The Cons

Helen D. Nolan, president of The Magnificent Doll, a New York City retail store specializing in antique and imported dolls and a partner and creative director of Della Temina, Travisano and Partners ad agency, told us she didn't believe in mentors! She wrote: "The concept of mentors as necessary opposes the idea that women learn to become self-sufficient and self-reliant entities. Until they do, I don't think they should *expect* to be respected in business."

Research Results

Ms. Nolan most definitely holds a minority opinion. Our survey found that the vast majority of successful female managers believe that mentors are essential.[3] This contention is supported by an abundance of research findings for both men and women. For example, Johnson found that most successful business people (men and women) have had at least one mentor.[4] In fact, it has been said that the lack of a mentor may be a major developmental handicap.[5] Men who thrive in large organizations are most likely to have had the support of bosses who took a special interest in their careers. Roche, as well as Borman, found that executives who have had a mentor earn more money at an earlier age, are better educated, and are more likely to follow a successful career path than those without one.[6]

If it is a necessity for a man to have a mentor to be successful, it may be even more essential for a woman. It has even been stated that, to reach top-level management positions, fatherlike sponsors are a necessity for women without family connections.[7]

WHAT CAN A MENTOR DO FOR THE WOMAN MANAGER?

One of the first questions a manager might ask is: What can a mentor do for me? A great deal of research has been done on this topic, and most of the conclusions are that mentors do a lot.[8] Our survey responses from 85 successful middle- and upper-middle-level women managers contained answers that were strikingly similar. When asked what exactly their mentors did for them, they replied:

My mentor was most helpful to me in the area of . . .

- ◆ learning how to deal with my male counterparts.
- ◆ developing my knowledge of the industry and actual recommendations for promotion.
- ◆ creating positions and opportunities for me.
- ◆ encouraging me to shoot for higher goals.

- helping me understand my weaknesses and guarding against passing the buck when the challenge was tough.
- understanding policy making.
- introducing me to the ins and outs of corporate politics, criticizing me constructively, and advising me as to my worth so as to give me self-confidence.
- overcoming others' resentment and objections to my being a woman manager.
- encouraging and providing me opportunities to test new skills.
- pointing out what I had to offer to those less observant.
- sticking his neck out to promote me—before it was fashionable.
- overcoming discouragement.
- giving me jobs I had never done, trusting me, and letting me do them.
- reinforcing my belief in my own capabilities.
- helping my career advancement.
- inspiring me to be more creative.
- keeping me and my performance visible to senior management and always giving credit for my work.

As can be derived from these responses, the mentor usually fulfills the role of coach or godfather. Both are equally important.

The Mentor's Role as Coach

As a coach, the mentor can help develop a manager's political and diplomatic skills. A female vice-president of a major utility company said she had a boss who served as a mentor by coaching her early in her career. She said:

I remember that before going to my first week-long conference out of town, he sat down with me and we discussed such things as what to wear and how to handle the cocktail hour. These little social things can be a problem, much as we don't like to admit it; and it's important to have somebody to turn to.

Another example of coaching is told by a young woman manager in a Midwest financial institution. "Once I nailed a senior vice-president during a meeting, pointing out that something he had stated as a fact was wrong," she recalls. "My boss pulled me aside after the meeting and told me never, never to correct a senior officer in an open forum again. He told me that if I wanted to set him straight I should tell my boss, who might tell his, so that the criticism would come from the same level or above." This type of coaching is typical of the mentoring relationship.

A mentor may spend considerable time counseling the protégée about managerial style, organizational culture, and personal style. One corporate vice-president said this of his protégée: "I worked with her to correct her laugh, her clothes, her mannerisms. Women have so few role models. They can't follow their mothers' teachings and they don't have a Brooks Brothers. They have a lot of catching up to do."

The Mentor's Role as Godfather

Mentorship can also involve the function of "godfather." A godfather brings the protégée along, promotes her, and makes sure she gets rewards. The mentor watches out for her interests and will not promote her too fast or too far. Usually this mentor surfaces and gives her the "final kick" into upper level management. One corporate vice-president of finance told us:

> I was Cyril's right hand. I helped him and he always looked out for me . . . gave me a lot of credit. He was a very stimulating example. The deeper I got into the investment business, the more responsibilities I had. I got interested in the dynamics of money-making and found it fascinating. When Cyril had to retire early for health reasons, he insisted I replace him, despite the fact that all of the other VP's were at least 10 years older than I.

HOW TO FIND A MENTOR

Women starting out in their careers often ask, "How do I find a mentor?" A frequent complaint was expressed as follows by a first-level manager in an engineering firm:

> I've heard all the arguments about finding a mentor who can pull you up in the organization. But it isn't easy if you are a woman. First of all, most of the people in big jobs are male. They would prefer to sponsor a male. Some of them are afraid that, if they do sponsor a woman, somebody will think the two of them have something going on.

It is indeed more difficult for a woman than it is for a man to find a mentor in most large organizations. The characteristics the woman needs to succeed—enthusiasm, the right image, and working well with others—are also the same characteristics necessary to attract a suitable mentor. Men actively seek mentors and go where they are likely to be found. Women in similar situations can't afford to wait to be chosen. A new woman manager should actively seek a mentor. She should look for the people who are in a position to help get tasks accomplished and let them know she respects their ability and seeks their support. Ultimately the mentor selects individuals to sponsor. Far earlier, though, the wise game players have chosen where to work and to be at the right place at the right time. High-performing women who practice the career development strategies discussed below can increase their chances of finding suitable mentors.

Make Your Goals Known

People do not assume automatically that women want to get ahead. Roche discovered that most women found mentors during the sixth to tenth year of their careers.[9] He hypothesized that, since this is the period when many women decide to pursue a "career" rather than simply "work," they announce their new professional goals at this stage.

One of the ways to overcome barriers women face when finding a mentor is to convince potential mentors that they are committed to a permanent career. A mentor may not want to invest time in training a woman who may only be a temporary asset. Consequently, a mentor may see women as assistants, not successors. A woman needs to deal with this stereotype by confirming her seriousness about her career.

Seek High Visibility and Document Your Accomplishments

It is important for a woman manager to keep an accurate record of what she has accomplished for performance reviews and career discussions. She should let people know what she accomplishes in tactful ways such as writing "for your information" notes or asking advice on the follow-up strategy for her completed project. High-visibility assignments and projects wherein she will be seen by the "right" people are the best ones to seek out. Just doing a good job of using these techniques will get a manager the recognition she needs.

Use the Networking System

For many years men have comfortably and naturally helped each other get ahead in the business world. In recent years, women have also adopted the network route to career advancement (see Figure 4-1). Women who have previously relied almost exclusively on males to be mentors are now looking at influential women for support, guidance, and role modeling.[10] Many professional organizations now have a strong informal network for informing, sharing, guiding, and providing support. Most cities have groups of women who meet on a monthly basis in the evening, during lunch hours, and even for breakfast. These networking groups can be a source of encouragement and support for the woman who takes risks in her professional setting. Within this environment women can share, trust, and depend on one another.

FIGURE 4-1

EXAMPLES OF NETWORKING SYSTEMS

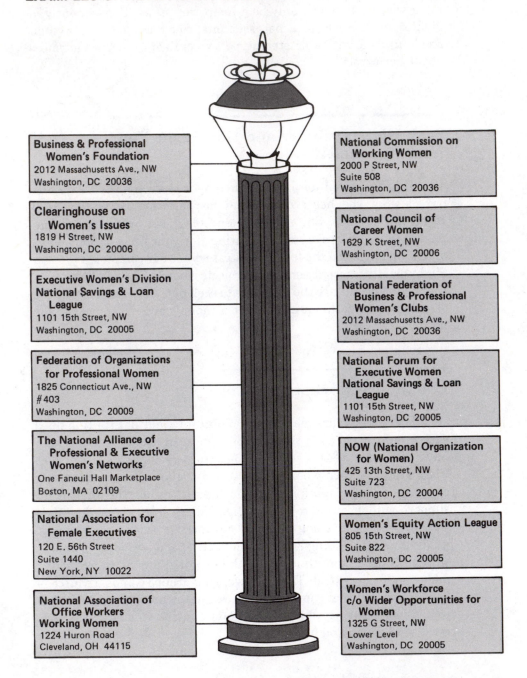

Business & Professional
  Women's Foundation
2012 Massachusetts Ave., NW
Washington, DC 20036

Clearinghouse on
  Women's Issues
1819 H Street, NW
Washington, DC 20006

Executive Women's Division
National Savings & Loan
  League
1101 15th Street, NW
Washington, DC 20005

Federation of Organizations
  for Professional Women
1825 Connecticut Ave., NW
#403
Washington, DC 20009

The National Alliance of
  Professional & Executive
  Women's Networks
One Faneuil Hall Marketplace
Boston, MA 02109

National Association for
  Female Executives
120 E. 56th Street
Suite 1440
New York, NY 10022

National Association of
  Office Workers
Working Women
1224 Huron Road
Cleveland, OH 44115

National Commission on
  Working Women
2000 P Street, NW
Suite 508
Washington, DC 20036

National Council of
  Career Women
1629 K Street, NW
Washington, DC 20006

National Federation of
  Business & Professional
  Women's Clubs
2012 Massachusetts Ave., NW
Washington, DC 20036

National Forum for
  Executive Women
National Savings & Loan
  League
1101 15th Street, NW
Washington, DC 20005

NOW (National Organization
  for Women)
425 13th Street, NW
Suite 723
Washington, DC 20004

Women's Equity Action League
805 15th Street, NW
Suite 822
Washington, DC 20005

Women's Workforce
c/o Wider Opportunities for
  Women
1325 G Street, NW
Lower Level
Washington, DC 20005

Remain Professional

In relationships with male superiors who may be potential mentors, a woman should at all times remain totally professional. It may be fun sometimes to be cute or flirtatious in relaxed situations, such as at lunchtime, but this image may carry on and detract from her effectiveness at work. If she flirts with her boss at lunch, he may have a difficult time viewing her as a competent professional when she is presenting a marketing plan to him later that afternoon. She should not send mixed messages about the image she is trying to project.

PROBLEMS ENCOUNTERED IN THE MENTOR RELATIONSHIP

Must a woman's mentor be male? Since there are more male managers, and they hold the more influential positions in organizations, most mentors are male. A male mentor with significant power and prestige of his own can be very effective in enhancing the prestige of a protégée. This type of "man's stamp of approval" makes a woman a more acceptable colleague or team member to her mostly male colleagues.

Being a mentor is an important cycle in men's lives.[11] Successful men express a sense of responsibility for "putting back into life what you get out," and many find satisfaction in being role models and developing talent.[12] However, some potential problems exist in the female/male mentor relationship that are absent from the male/male or the female/female mentor relationships.

Traditional Cultural Conditioning

Their traditional cultural conditioning causes many senior male executives to view women as wives, mothers, and sweethearts, but not as executive peers. Consequently, such men do not consider women to be appropriate subjects for the intensive time and effort required to bring them along in the executive ranks. They view other men as safe investments with a higher probability of success than women. Fortunately, as more and more women enter the managerial ranks, this stereotype is slowly changing. One male executive explained, "If you're going to create a topflight organization, you have to have topflight people. My chances of getting topflight people are halved without women. If other men are uncomfortable about this, that's their problem."

Sexual Attraction

Sex can be a dangerous hitch in an otherwise healthy mentor relationship.[13] Romantic or sexual interests confound the mentor relationship and may create conflicts and power struggles where there were none before. The male mentor/lover may, for example, instill in his protégée the notion that she cannot fulfill her talents without him in order to secure the relationship for his own needs.[14]

In view of the closeness of the mentor/protégée relationship, it is easy to see how romances develop. A woman may have sexual feelings toward a male mentor and he may be equally attracted to her. It is possible for them to deal with these feelings by talking about them as a difficulty in their professional relationship. Most women feel it is their responsibility to behave professionally and learn to cope with the inevitable tensions and rumors that arise. Some male mentors, fortunately, feel that the responsibility should be *shared*. "There is a greater tendency for sexual attachment when the mentor is supportive and the rest of the environment isn't. You'd be dumb not to think about sexual tension and rumors. It's always there. Professional conduct by both people is essential."[15]

The Servant Trap

If female protégées successfully avoid the sexual trap, they still have to watch out for the **servant trap**.[16] Men are used to having women serve them. As a result, they may ask a woman manager to do all kinds of work that is more fitting for someone in a lower position. It is sometimes difficult to refuse a demeaning task without seeming to reject one's superior. However, there are times when it may be necessary for a woman to sit down with her mentor and clarify her role and career expectations. It may be appropriate at this time to suggest that whatever tasks he has been asking her to do can be delegated to someone else in a more appropriate position.

As more women move into management positions and work side by side with men, men will no longer view them as sex objects and servants but as friends and colleagues. As men are freed of their stereotypes and consequent prejudices about women, women will be freed to enjoy equal recognition for their competence and equal power.

Difficulty in Letting Go

Another potential problem with a mentor relationship is the mentor's difficulty in letting go. Some women have felt that mentors behave like overprotective fathers holding them back instead of enhancing their careers. In these cases there is a need for the protégée to break away, become independent, and function on her own. Even the best of mentors must eventually be abandoned if the protégée is to become fully mature.[17]

CAN WOMEN BE MENTORS?

Unfortunately female mentors are hard to find. Today there are still too few women who are in the top positions and wield the necessary influence. If a woman is lucky enough to find a female mentor, the latter will have two additional qualities over those of a male mentor. She can be a role model for the protégée, and she will understand what it is like to be a woman in the protégée's position because she has probably been there herself.

A woman mentor fills a crying need. "There are problems that give you a sinking, sick feeling—like being the only female in a group of 60 males—that no man could ever understand," said an officer of a large metropolitan bank. "A woman mentor can be a tremendous help."

In the past, many women in the upper ranks of organizations

felt their positions were too precarious to permit them to help anyone else. Others were "Queen Bees" who, "in the face of all odds and
without the aid of affirmative action, have made it to the top." Many
of these women feel that "No one helped me, so why should I help
others?" Josefowitz explains the Queen Bee syndrome as follows:

> People who have gone through especially severe
> organizational initiation rites seem to impose upon new
> entrants similar, equally difficult experiences. In other
> words, if they had to earn their stripes the hard way, they
> will see to it that others do the same. To institutionalize a
> painful experience gives it value simply because not to do
> so would devalue and diminish that membership. No one
> wants to place less significance on a particularly painful
> experience. Perhaps this is what the Queen Bee contends
> with. The expectation is that the younger and inexperi-
> enced people should be mirror images of the Queen Bees
> and, therefore, should go through the same experiences.[18]

All organizations have "rites of passage" or an initiation period
that every newcomer has to go through. However, these need not be
the same rites experienced by women who entered years ago and
fought all the odds. The problems faced by women beginning managerial careers today are not the same, but they are still difficult.
Many people recognize this. As the growing number of women in
high-ranking corporate posts pushes other women closer to equity
with male colleagues, female mentors have begun to appear in more
abundance. Many executive women now make being a mentor to
younger women part of their goals. Organized networking groups of
professional women have grown by leaps and bounds in the past five
years. These groups attempt to fill the function of the male's "old
boys' network" by providing professional information, support, references, information about job openings, and emotional nurturance.

ACTION GUIDELINES

People need support from others throughout their lives. This is not
any less critical for career women in facilitating their movement into top-
management positions. Mentors, both male and female, are a primary

source of this vital support. Nevertheless, a woman has the original and continuing responsibility for her career development.

Things a woman can do to help herself and her mentor include:

1. Developing a clear understanding of how people get ahead in her organization.
2. Clarifying the kind of support she needs and expects.
3. Communicating effectively her expectations to people who can help her.
4. Establishing a support system which contributes to both her personal and organizational effectiveness.

FOOTNOTES

1. Mary Cunningham, *Powerplay: What Really Happened at Bendix* (New York: Simon and Schuster, 1984).

2. Ruth Halcomb, "Mentors and the Successful Woman," *Across the Board* (February, 1980), pp. 13-18.

3. Johanna S. Hunsaker, "The Mentor Relationship: Fact or Fiction" (From a paper presented at the annual meeting of the Academy of Management, New York, August 16, 1982).

4. Mary C. Johnson, "Mentors: The Key to Development and Growth," *Training and Development Journal* (July, 1980), pp. 55-57.

5. Daniel J. Levinson, *The Seasons of a Man's Life* (New York: Knopf, 1978), pp. 40-63.

6. Gerald R. Roche, "Much Ado About Mentors," *Harvard Business Review* (January/February, 1979), pp. 14-15, 20-28. See also C. Borman and S. Colson, "Mentoring: An Effective Career Guidance Technique," *The Vocational Guidance Journal*, Vol. 3 (1984), pp. 192-197.

7. Margaret Hennig and Anne Jardim, *The Managerial Woman* (New York: Doubleday, 1977), p. 120.

8. Ruth Halcomb, *op. cit.*, pp. 13-18. See also Mary F. Cook, "Is the Mentor Relationship Primarily a Male Experience?" *Personnel Administrator* (November, 1979), p. 40; Eileen C. Shapiro, Florence P. Haseltine, and Mary P. Rowe, "Moving Up: Role Models, Mentors, and the Patron System," *Sloan Management Review* (Spring 1978), pp. 51-58.

9. Gerald R. Roche, *op. cit.*, pp. 14-15, 20-28.

10. Philomena D. Warichay, "The Climb to the Top: Is the Network the Route for Women?" *The Personnel Administrator* (April, 1980), pp. 72-80.

11. Daniel J. Levinson, *op. cit.*, pp. 40-63.

12. Lawton Fitt and Derek Newton, "When the Mentor Is a Man and the Protégée a Woman," *Harvard Business Review* (March/April, 1981), pp. 56-60.

13. Gail Sheehy, "The Mentor Connection: The Secret Link in the Successful Woman's Life," *New York Magazine* (April, 1976), p. 90.

14. Ruth Halcomb, *op. cit.*, pp. 13-18.

15. Fitt and Newton, *op. cit.*, pp. 56-60.

16. Natasha Josefowitz, *Paths to Power: A Woman's Guide from First Job to Top Executive* (Reading, MA: Addison-Wesley Publishing Company, 1980), pp. 93-95.

17. Gail Sheehy, *Passages: Predictable Crises of Adult Life* (New York: E. P. Dutton and Company, 1974), p. 151.

18. Natasha Josefowitz, *op. cit.*, p. 98.

CHAPTER 5

Managing Yourself

OUTLINE

I. Stress Management
   A. Sources of Stress
      1. Uncertainty
      2. Lack of Control
      3. Pressure
   B. Methods of Dealing with Stress
      1. Coping Techniques
      2. Adaptation Techniques

II. Time Management
   A. Time-Management Techniques
      1. Establish Priorities
      2. Control Time Wasters
   B. Other Timesaving Ideas

III. Career Management
   A. Meanings of "Career"
   B. Steps in Career Planning
      1. Know Yourself
      2. Set Specific Goals
   C. Barriers to Career Development
      1. Low Initial Challenge
      2. Low Self-Actualization Satisfaction
      3. Lack of Regular Performance Appraisal
      4. Unrealistically High Aspirations
      5. Inability to Create Challenge
      6. Threat to Superiors
   D. Realistic Job Previews
   E. Problems of—and Strategies for—Reentry Women
      1. Competition with Younger Women
      2. Relating to Younger Supervisors
   F. Strategies for Career Advancement
   G. Basic Everyday Tactics
   H. EEO Guidelines to Know
      1. Changes Effected by EEOA
      2. What to Do If Faced with Discrimination

Action Guidelines

> I can put the wash on the line, feed the kids, get
> dressed, pass out the kisses, and get to work by 5 of 9:00—
> 'cause I'm a wo-man.

So went the TV jingle for Enjoli, the "8-hour perfume for the 24-hour woman." Today's career woman, however, often finds herself trapped by the superwoman squeeze. She experiences constant pressure attempting to juggle her career with her personal life, family life, and social life (if she has one). Unlike the career woman portrayed in the Enjoli perfume commercial, today's career woman often finds herself hardly able to catch her breath as she tries to fulfill her multiple obligations.

The women who pursue careers in management must constantly be on the alert, scouting the territory for potential problems. The basic self-management skills that can help women managers cope more effectively with their multiple responsibilities pertain to the areas of (1) stress management, (2) time management, and (3) career management. Each of these is discussed below.

STRESS MANAGEMENT

Several definitions of stress have been offered over the years, but the most direct way of defining it is, "In its medical sense, **stress** is essentially the rate of wear and tear on the body."[1]

Many women accept stress as inevitable; it is the "price you pay" for having a career. Other women don't anticipate stress, and they learn the hard way that managing a career and a personal life is an extremely demanding job. Only after being pushed to the brink of collapse do they recognize the need to manage their lives in ways that minimize stress and maximize performance and satisfaction. This is what **stress management** is all about—the ability to manage the forces in people's lives rather than having these forces control them.

All people need some stress in their lives. Stress can be *functional* by activating and enhancing one's performance. For example, a dry mouth and a tight stomach before an important presentation often help a manager to do a good job. But too much stress can become *dysfunctional*. Too many tight stomachs may cause the manager to develop a bleeding ulcer. Beyond a certain point, too much stress overloads the body's system and performance decreases. The female body is warned of too much stress through such symptoms as chest pain, menstrual disorder, sore neck or back, headache, bad breath, insomnia, excessive sleep, or stomach pain. As a matter of fact, stress can produce abnormal reactions and it can even kill humans.

When people make too many demands on themselves, they experience physiological, emotional, and psychological changes that are called the "stress response." The body reacts to stress by pumping hormones into the blood stream where they go into action. The body's response is essentially the same whether the stress results from playing a game of bridge, surviving a frightening accident on the freeway, going to an important meeting, or running a race.

Whether or not a person experiences a stress response depends on how the person perceives and responds to the demands of the environment. Not all events produce stress for everyone. But those events that are perceived as threatening do. They are called **stressors**.

Different situations can be more or less stress-producing for different people. People also differ in terms of their ability to tolerate stress; and an individual's stress tolerance varies over time. Each time people do experience stress, their bodies need time to adapt and to restore their equilibrium.

The issue of energy and health is often overlooked by women managers. In the rush of establishing a career in what is essentially a man's world, they often ignore important parts of their private lives such as recreation and health maintenance. This is not a good idea. Much has been written about heart attacks and ulcers commonly suffered by male managers. It is dangerous for managerial women to assume that they are somehow immune to the wear and tear that similar careers may have on their health. Women who work full time are subject to the same stress and strain as men. Women workers also have to get up in the morning, fight traffic, climb on subways, worry about deadlines, work for promotions, and like men, they sometimes go home and take out their problems on their families. Working women are subject to the same illnesses as men: heart disease, high blood pressure, ulcers, and increasing rates of alcoholism. It is well known that the managerial life-style provides an environment that is high in stress.

Stress appears to be inevitable for women managers. The women we interviewed suffered from stress, and they revealed their symptoms in the following responses:

- ◆ "I've had a constant nervous stomach since I took this senior vice-presidency."
- ◆ "I eat like a big pig when I am under stress at work. Pressures and deadlines on me mean ten extra pounds."
- ◆ "I get very tired. I go to bed early, but then I wake up in the middle of the night and think of all the work I need to do."

Sources of Stress

Uncertainty, lack of control, and pressure are common sources of stress for all managers. Middle-management women are probably gulping Alka-Seltzer as much as middle-management men do.

Uncertainty. *New* women managers, in particular, experience much stress because they live with perpetual ambiguity and uncertainty. Often they are one of a few women in their positions, and their jobs lack clear definitions of responsibilities or expectations of performance.

Many working women who have children bear a double burden. They have problems associated with the reliability of their baby-sitters, the health of their children, and baking cookies for the PTA. In each instance, there is the constant fear that at any time something may happen to upset the status quo.

Lack of Control. Another source of stress related to uncertainty is lack of control. Part of the stress-inducing quality of uncertain or unpredictable events is that people have no control over them. At other times, although people do know what is going to happen, they can't do what is necessary to meet the demand. They may know what the proper solution is, but they are powerless to control other people or the events necessary to bring about the desired outcome. For example, it can be extremely stressful working for a supervisor who changes plans abruptly or springs last-minute rush assignments on a subordinate.

__Pressure.__ Pressure is a source of stress which involves how a person evaluates and feels about an event. Consider the difference between meeting a deadline on a project important to a manager's career—one that may result in a promotion—and meeting a deadline on a routine project. Although the real pressure of each project may be the same and may cause just as many disruptions in her work or home life, she is likely to experience them in very different ways. The first project has more riding on it, but the pressure is a turn-on—it is as exciting as it is stressful! The second project, because it lacks excitement and value, is purely stress producing.

Methods of Dealing with Stress

How can one manage stress in a productive way and avoid its negative outcomes? There are several stress-reducing techniques which have been proven to be useful. But first it helps to recognize that there is a difference between coping techniques and adaptation techniques.[2] **Coping techniques** help a person to live with the problem, while **adaptation techniques** solve the problem by modifying either the sources of stress or the person's reactions to them. In order to manage stress, the manager has to find ways to modify the situations that cause stress, as well as her ways of responding to stress.

__Coping Techniques.__ The coping techniques generally involve things that seem to help people get through a stressful time. The most common coping technique involves the use of drugs or alcohol. One study found that 40 percent of the sample of senior female executives had been or were still taking tranquilizers, antidepressants, and sleeping pills as a means of relieving tension.[3] At the middle level of management, the number of women on Valium and related drugs was about 30 percent. Because of the stresses of a dual career and their own inner achievement pressure, some women managers found themselves thinking about work during their "own" time. One of them said, "I find very often my brain ticking over like mad at night and I can't sleep . . . I take Valium then, but never during the day."

Another way some managers cope with stress is to drink alcohol. Neither alcohol nor drugs, however, relieves stress. They may temporarily mask the feelings a person experiences, but they do not change the stress-producing event or the person's feelings about it. In many cases, the use of drugs or alcohol only compounds problems and leads to dependence, addiction, poorer performance, and physical deterioration.

Adaptation Techniques. The adaptation techniques have more positive effects although they still do not eliminate dysfunctional stress on a permanent basis.

Regular physical exercise is one such method. There is much evidence that regular exercise has multiple benefits for physical and mental health. Unfortunately, many women do not find the time for physical exercise. In addition, many females were not socialized as children to incorporate exercise as a regular part of their life-style. This is unfortunate because it has long been recognized by medical authorities that certain types of pent-up frustration, anxiety, and stress may be released through physical exertion. The rapid rise in heart attacks and strokes among young Americans has been an instrumental factor in bringing about a significant increase in physical activity such as jogging, bicycle riding, aerobic dancing, jazz exercising, and walking. The female manager can utilize exercise as a way of building physical strength, as well as releasing tension and anxiety.

Recreation is another method for escaping from situations that bring about stress. Taking vacations, going to the movies, or doing whatever the manager really likes to do provides a chance to relax and renew her system for dealing with the stressful situation again.

Relaxation exercises are other ways of giving the manager some positive time out. There are a wide variety of techniques, methods, and approaches to becoming more in touch with oneself at different levels of consciousness. Perhaps the most well-known of these techniques is Transcendental Meditation (TM).[4] Other techniques include biofeedback, general relaxation, meditation, and yoga.[5] These techniques can be extremely valuable in teaching the manager how to remove herself temporarily from a tension-producing environment or to relieve frustration and anxiety. One telephone company supervisor who meditates every afternoon stated, "When I get back from meditation, I am not only more effective, but I get along better with people and myself too. I am much more productive." This is an example of how "spending time creates time!" Spending some time to relax revitalizes the manager, allowing her to become more productive than she would be if she had continued to perform under stress.

There are many other strategies that the manager can employ to help reduce the level of regularly experienced stress or, at the very least, to help cope with continuing high stress. A few further examples are given below:

1. Increase her *self-awareness* of how she behaves on the job. She can find out what are her own limits and recognize signs of potential trouble. Learning when to withdraw from a situation and when to seek help from others on the job are often effective strategies to relieve stress.

2. Develop *outside interests* to take her mind off work. This solution is particularly important for high-achieving, hard-driving people whose physical health may depend on toning down their relentless drive for success.

3. Try to find a variety of personal or *unique solutions* for coping with stress. One savings and loan executive described how she reacts to stressful situations. "I walk into my office, close the door, and pound the hell out of my typewriter, saying all of the things on paper that I want to say. It works every time. Then I rip up the paper and throw it in the trash can."

4. Identify what specific things cause stress in her life. In order to do something about stress, she first has to *identify its source*. Then it may be possible to eliminate or modify it.

5. Schedule her life so that *conflicting demands* can be avoided. This is important on both a lifetime and a day-to-day basis.

6. *Plan* her career. She shouldn't just assume that things will work out. Often they don't; and if they do, they won't always be in directions she prefers.

7. Try to *reduce uncertainty* as much as possible by establishing a regular routine for those things within her control.
   Then she won't have to worry about when to do what.

TIME MANAGEMENT

A major contribution to stress for managerial women is the
lack of sufficient time to get everything done in their lives. **Overload** (too much to do in the time available) and **multiple roles**
(being responsible for many different kinds of activities) are usually
to blame. These are inherent in managerial positions and can be
overwhelming at times. OSHA (Occupational Safety and Health
Administration) listed the job of "manager" as the number one high-
stress job in a study conducted for the Department of Health, Education and Welfare.[6] Using time effectively can be a major step in
handling the stress and multiple demands of the managerial role.

Many matters reaching a manager's desk demand substantial
blocks of time, and there is seldom enough time to do everything
fully or effectively. Time is a scarce, precious, and irretrievable
resource. Unlike money, human resources, or raw materials, time
cannot be accumulated. People are forced to spend time, whether
they choose to or not. They can, however, determine the way in
which they spend it. Like other resources, time is either misman-
aged or it is handled effectively.

Many managers do not use their time wisely. They fail to
match their time with their most important responsibilities, and
they won't acknowledge the fact that it is possible to take control
and learn to utilize time more effectively. While a manager can't
manufacture more time, she can learn to make better use of the time
she has. As is often said, managing time does not mean working
harder—it just means working smarter!

For the woman manager this problem is especially crucial. She
not only faces the overwhelming demands of her managerial assignments, but also often has multiple commitments. Women in management often have the responsibility of a job and a family (another
full-time job) simultaneously, whereas men in comparable positions
usually have wives who assume the traditional role of caring for the

family. Culture has conditioned most people to believe that the home is the woman's responsibility. Unless she has a husband who shares equally in family responsibilities, she has two jobs in contrast to a male peer's one. Whoever asked a man how he manages to combine marriage and family with a career? How many career women have expressed the wish that they had a "wife"? How many times could the woman manager have used one herself?

Studies show that employed women generally get little help with the housework from their husbands.[7] To combine two time-consuming careers, a woman has to become an expert manager of her time. If she wants to compete successfully with her male counterparts, she needs to seek efficient ways to juggle her office and home routines.

The women managers we surveyed tend to manage their time well. One successful woman in the savings and loan industry pointed out that "managing my time is important not only for controlling my stress level, but also because others are watching me, making sure I'm not wasting my time on frivolous conversations and gossip!"

Many male managers are conditioned by the myth that women waste time pursuing frivolous activities. The woman manager must work to overcome this myth. Effective management of time is a potent demonstration of competence which can dispel the foundation of this negative stereotype.

Time-Management Techniques

One of the most useful approaches to effective time management is described by Alan Lakein in his book, *How to Get Control of Your Time and Your Life*.[8] Basic to his system is learning how to plan what one wants to do and then organizing one's use of time to get it done. "Time is a constant that cannot be altered . . . . We cannot manage time itself. We can only manage our activities with respect to it." In other words, managing time, like managing stress, involves learning to manage one's own behavior.

Two of the most common time-management techniques are (1) to establish priorities, and (2) to control time wasters. Other strategies for time management will also be presented in this section.

Establish Priorities. Whether the manager is planning for today or next year, she needs to establish her priorities. She has to identify and concentrate on the tasks of the highest priority and eliminate low-priority activities.

Lakein suggests using the simple *ABC Priority System.*[9] It works like this: The manager should plan her daily work by listing everything she needs to do today. She should write a capital "A" next to those items on the list that have a high value (the things that are really important), a "B" for those with medium value, and a "C" for those with low value. She gets the most out of her time by doing the A's first, and saving the B's and C's for later. When she has a sense of what her A goals are, she can begin to plan her time to accomplish them.

ABC's are relative, depending on one's point of view. The A tasks generally will stand out in contrast to B and C tasks. A person's ABC's may change over time. Today's A may become tomorrow's C, while today's C may become tomorrow's A. The manager needs to set priorities continually, always considering the *best use of her time right now.* When she begins to feel overwhelmed and frustrated, she should remind herself that "there is always enough time for the important things." After all, what difference does it really make if a C task does not get done? She should ask herself, "Would anything terrible happen if I didn't do this item?" If the answer is no, then she shouldn't do it.

Control Time Wasters. A **time waster** is an event, incident, or situation that, if repeated often, tends to eat into one's time. Although a time waster is not necessarily always wasteful or undesirable, the manager may wish that it didn't take so much of her managerial time—time that she could use more profitably on more significant aspects of her job. Some common situations that *can* become time wasters are: meetings, correspondence, visitors, reports, questionnaires, committee work, complaints, employee grievances, lost materials or records, "emergency" situations, telephone calls, overinvolvement in a subordinate's personal problems, community activities, appointments, late arrivals, lack of delegation, interruptions, and pet projects.

The manager should take several minutes to consider what her time wasters are. After listing them, she should take a closer look and ask herself some questions. Which of her time wasters are generated internally by her? Which are generated externally by events or other people? Which could she control or eliminate? What has she done, attempted to do, or what does she plan to do about these time wasters?

Other Timesaving Ideas

By sharpening her awareness of her use of time, the manager can control and create more time for herself. Some further timesaving ideas for her include the following:

1. Keeping a daily "THINGS TO DO TODAY" list and reviewing it each morning.

2. Blocking off time for priority activities—either save a time slot in each day or set a day aside each week.

3. Not letting anything interfere with priority time.

4. Assigning priorities based on value/time ratios.

5. Scheduling appointments, but always reserving at least one hour a day of uncommitted time.

6. Handling paper only once; don't keep reshuffling it.

7. Not procrastinating—if something has to be done, do it immediately.

8. Delegating as much as possible to others. Unless the manager absolutely has to do something herself, she should assign it to someone else.

9. Learning to know her "prime time." When does she work best? She should save her prime time for priority projects.

10. Trying to be flexible. The manager should always leave time in her schedule for emergencies or catching up.

11. Planning time to relax. If she is exhausted, she won't be able to work effectively or efficiently.

12. Learning to use transition time to get things done. For example, does she read, catch the news on radio, or discuss matters with her husband and family while she dresses, does her nails, or eats breakfast? How does she use her time spent in commuting, coffee breaks, lunch hour, or waiting in offices? Does she carry her list with her so that she can use time to plan? Does she carry paper and pencil for writing or does she have something to read?

13. Turning C activities into things that can be put off indefinitely. How many C activities does she do that, in the end, don't have to be done or can be done later if they turn out to be important? She should learn to discriminate and put them aside.

By taking a hard, close look at how she is presently using her time, the manager may surprise herself. She may find that she is doing things that don't need to be done at all. She may be able to delegate other things, thus leaving herself free for all those activities which only she can handle.

Beyond the strategies already mentioned for managing time well, there is another essential guideline for the manager. She must invest time in order to make time, and considerable time must be invested in herself. The solution does not lie in forfeiting a rich and complex life. As Baruch, Barnett, and Rivers point out in their book *Lifeprints: New Patterns of Love and Work for Today's Woman*, multiple roles and demands benefit women. Those women with both careers and families have a greater sense of well-being than women who have only one or neither.[10]

CAREER MANAGEMENT

The last area of self-management to be discussed in this book is career management. The manager can achieve career success and satisfaction if she has the appropriate information on career opportunities and follows through with a planned development effort. This takes training, skills, and an awareness of job requirements and opportunities.

The majority of women tend to focus on their present jobs with little long-term career planning. Many women think, "If I just do my job, the company will take care of my career." This just doesn't happen! Compare this frame of mind to the comments we received from a 36-year-old vice-president of a large utilities company:

> Everything that has happened in my career has been planned. I set goals in college and at each job. My goals were not narrow or restrictive; I developed alternatives for advancement at each level. For example, in one mid-level managerial position, my alternatives were (1) to get promoted to the vice-president's position within five years, or (2) to get a comparable promotion in another department within five years, or (3) to get a position with a higher salary and responsibility in another organization. I always had options, and I was constantly working on them. I believe a woman can make her own breaks in life. It is hard work, but we do have some control over our destinies.

The above approach to career development is almost textbook perfect! This vice-president was prepared, was flexible, and assessed multiple options.

Meanings of "Career"

The concept of career has many meanings. The most popular and accepted meaning is reflected in the following definitions: moving upward; making more money; having more responsibility; and acquiring more status, more prestige, and more power. Although people can think of mothers and volunteers as having careers, this book deals with careers in occupations and professions. A commonly accepted definition of **career** is "the individually perceived sequence of attitudes and behaviors associated with work-related experiences and activities over the span of a person's life.[11] This definition emphasizes that the long-term career does not imply success or failure except in the individual's judgment. The career consists of both attitude and behaviors and is an ongoing sequence of work-related activities.

Steps in Career Planning

To increase the chances of career success and satisfaction, one important step to be taken is *self-motivated* career planning. For the woman manager, it means taking the initiative and responsibility to plan her career.

Know Yourself. One of the first steps in career planning is for the manager to know herself. This means having an appreciation of her strengths, accomplishments, and desires. To get to know herself better, she should think about herself, her goals and aspirations, and her work life. She should write out several separate answers to the question: "Who am I?" Then she should write several separate statements about "Things I would like to accomplish." The woman manager should make her statements as specific and concise as possible. Then the statements should be ranked in the order of their importance to her (see Figure 5-1).

FIGURE 5-1

EXERCISE 1—KNOW YOURSELF

Who Am I?	Things I Would Like to Accomplish
I am	I would like to ....
I am	I would like to ....
I am	I would like to ....

These self-perception exercises can generate data for self-assessment of the manager's skills, accomplishments, weaknesses, aspirations, satisfactions, and values. They provide a starting point for developing her vision of the future—which is necessary for goal setting—and taking action to achieve her goals.

Set Specific Goals. The next step in career planning is to set specific goals. The increased likelihood of change resulting from the setting and articulation of goals is well documented. Goal setting clarifies the situation and focuses on specific issues. A manager's chances of finding career satisfaction increase if she establishes clear-cut goals.

Occupational floundering is the result of *not* setting realistic goals. This occurs when an individual enters the labor force without a firm commitment to an occupational goal. To help focus on setting specific career goals, the manager should write out different responses to the following statement: "Five years from now I will be satisfied if . . ." Then, for each of the goals she has just listed, she should complete this statement: "To accomplish this goal I will . . ." (see Figure 5-2).

FIGURE 5-2

EXERCISE 2—SET SPECIFIC GOALS

Five Years From Now I Will Be Satisfied If	To Accomplish This Goal, I Will
. . . .	. . . .
. . . .	. . . .
. . . .	. . . .

The product of a manager's work in the preceding exercises is a set of prioritized goals and strategies for achieving them based on self-assessment. Conceptualizing life goals that project future alternatives is something women traditionally have not done. Goal setting, however, is a crucial aspect of career development.

Barriers to Career Development

From the moment new employees enter the organization, they are given cues about the quality of performance that is expected and rewarded. Most new employees are motivated to be accepted into this new social system and they are more receptive to cues from their environment than they ever will be again. However, many new employees—both men and women—will suffer from the **reality shock syndrome**, which is the disparity between initial job expectations and the hard realities of what the job actually entails. This can be unpleasant, disconcerting, and depressing. This clash between expectations and reality has been called "reality shock."[12] According to Hall, there are six factors that contribute to the reality shock syndrome. They are: (1) low initial challenge, (2) low self-actualization satisfaction, (3) lack of regular performance appraisal, (4) unrealistically high aspirations, (5) inability to create challenge, and (6) threat to superiors. Each of these factors is discussed below.

Low Initial Challenge. Both the job search and the recruitment process are "selling" jobs in many ways. The female applicant presents her best side and emphasizes her strong points, but so does the company. Recruiters often *overstate* the promise and challenge of the first job in order to attract the most desirable and promising candidates. Actually, however, most organizations start employees out on a relatively easy project and only gradually increase the difficulty of the projects as the employees gain experience.

It is easy for a woman who is just starting on a job to feel that she is the victim of discrimination *because* she is female. She should look around at other trainees to see if they are in the same position. It may be that all new employees' expectations for early job challenges are going unfulfilled. If this is *not* the case, she should *document* this situation and follow through with the procedure which will be described on page 107 for dealing with discrimination.

Low Self-Actualization Satisfaction. Recruiters, again in the zest and zeal of their sales jobs, promise growth and self-fulfillment on the job. More often than not, however, an organization rewards conformity to its customs and standard operating procedures. Very few organizations reward creativity on entry-level jobs. If the applicant finds that she really desires more independence, it may be better for her to adapt to an organization for a short period of time and leave when she feels that she has gained appropriate experience if promotional opportunities are not forthcoming.

Lack of Regular Performance Appraisal. Most people feel that performance appraisal is necessary to motivate and train new employees. Thus, regular feedback on performance is promised to most new personnel. However, many managers perform this appraisal poorly with new employees or neglect it altogether. Their performance appraisal may simply consist of, "You're doing a fine job; keep it up." Consequently, new people in the organization are left in a state of confusion as to how well they are really doing and how they can improve.

Unrealistically High Aspirations. Many new employees begin work eager to apply the modern skills and techniques that they have been taught. They feel that they already have the ability to perform at levels well above their entry-level position. In fact, however, these new employees are generally unskilled in practical applications and realities of the work world, and their high aspirations and "classroom theories" are often resented by others in the organization. No superior likes being made to feel that a skill he or she is utilizing is already outdated. Thus, the fact that their superiors might not rate them quite as high as they rate themselves comes as a rude awakening to many new employees.

Inability to Create Challenge. Despite the fact that first jobs are usually not terribly challenging, they can often be made more that way if new employees have the initiative to create challenges on their own. This doesn't just automatically happen; in fact, it doesn't happen very often. Most people neglect to take a more active role in personally defining their jobs, and most managers assign newly hired people to "safe" jobs. If the female applicant is willing to be creative, she should _ask_ for challenges—for more difficult and complex tasks.

Threat to Superiors. A newcomer fresh out of technical school, college, or graduate school may bring more expertise to a job than the superior possesses. In addition, the newcomer may be entering the organization at a salary that is much higher than the superior's initial salary was. Thus, some superiors may regard the young employee as a threat so that the supervisor/subordinate relationship may be somewhat strained.

Realistic Job Previews

To create more realistic expectations and to combat the high turnover rate caused by reality shock, many organizations are giving their applicants and new employees realistic job previews. It isn't fair to the individual or to the organization to "sell" something that simply is not there in the first job. By giving realistic job previews, recruits are informed about both the positive and negative aspects of the job for which they have applied. A young female MBA fresh out of college might be told, for example, that she will be watched quite carefully on initial projects because it is her first job, rather than be given a large amount of independence. Or the recruiter might point out that while the administrative and paperwork burden is boring, dull, and tiresome, it is still a necessity for certain jobs. By providing realistic job previews, applicants form realistic initial expectations and thus do not develop too much dissatisfaction with the actual situations they encounter.

Several studies have shown that realistic job expectations lead to decreased employee turnover. Moreover, job acceptance rates do not appear to be lower for applicants exposed to unfavorable information about the job than they are for recruits exposed only to positive job information.

In summary, two aspects of the individual's early job experiences appear especially critical: the match of expectations with initial job assignment and the supportive behavior of the individual's first supervisor. Thus, a female employee's early job experiences and the type of supervisory behavior she has been subjected to appear to be particularly important in influencing her adjustment to the organization and subsequent career success.

Problems of and Strategies for Reentry Women

A major adjustment to the organization is faced by the "mid-life" woman who is either returning to the work force after a substantial time of child rearing or who has never held full-time paid employment. The number of midlife women reentering the work force has steadily increased in recent years. One reason is that the women's movement has opened job opportunities. Second, the increased divorce rate has made it necessary for many women to take over primary financial support of their families. Third, many families require two incomes just to keep pace with inflation.

The reentry woman faces special problems that do not apply to the young female who has just graduated from college. Some unique problems that reentry women might face are (1) competition with younger women, and (2) difficulty relating to younger supervisors. The woman manager should be sensitive to this unique position, whether she fills it herself or must relate to those who do.

Competition with Younger Women.

Midlife women are often overly concerned that they are unequal competition to their younger counterparts. Younger women are commonly thought of as being more physically attractive and, therefore, may have a better chance of being hired and promoted rapidly. The more mature women, on the other hand, are thought of as having a better record of attendance and punctuality and as representing a lower turnover risk. Neither of these commonly held views is particularly true, however, and the final outcome of competition is usually based on competence.

Relating to Younger Supervisors.

It is a substantial change for many midlife women to be supervised by males or females who are young enough to be their children. Adjustments have to be made in both directions. Young supervisors sometimes feel awkward supervising women old enough to be their mothers. Exposure to the situation seems to be the best cure for such feelings of awkwardness.

Another helpful approach to bridging the age gap in such relationships is for the midlife women to recognize that today technical qualifications and job experience determine the balance of authority. In a work setting, age is a weak source of authority compared to experience and job competence.

Strategies for Career Advancement

There are numerous strategies for advancing the woman manager's career. Schoonmaker proposes the following nine-step career strategy:[13]

1. *Accept the fact that there are some inescapable and irreconcilable conflicts between the woman manager and the organization.* Personal goals enter heavily into the formulation of career goals. Ideally, there is an integration of career and personal goals, but things don't always work out ideally.

Sometimes career goals have to be modified to fit personal goals; sometimes the opposite is true. What is good for the organization is not always good for the manager. She must recognize the need to *watch out for herself.*

2. *Accept the fact that the boss may be essentially indifferent to her career objectives.* Though it is ideal to have a mentor who cares about her and her career, the woman manager should be prepared for the fact that this may not occur. She should be prepared to *practice self-nomination.* She should have the courage and assertiveness to ask for what she wants—a promotion, a raise, or a transfer—because her boss may not believe that she is actually seeking more responsibility. Indeed, many more people claim to be seeking advancement than the number who will actually accept more responsibility. The manager is the person responsible for her own career. Facing this fact will allow her to act in her own interests.

3. *Establish clear-cut goals to increase the chances of finding career satisfaction.* The manager should establish a timetable and reevaluate her goals as time progresses.

4. *Analyze her assets and liabilities.* What can the manager do well? What does she enjoy doing? One of the most vital ingredients in her successful career planning is to have an accurate picture of her strengths, weaknesses, and preferences. It is foolish for her not to take advantage of her abilities and unrealistic to pursue goals that require abilities she does not have. Realistic career goals should enable her to operate from a position of strength.

5. *Stay tuned to the outside world to heighten her sensitivity to the external environment—to be aware of and to analyze opportunities.* Just as organizations must adapt to their external environment, so must individuals. Career advancement can be enhanced by preparing for a career in a growth area. Some ways to accomplish this are by carefully studying basic courses, reviewing secondary sources such as *The Wall Street Journal*, personal observations, and tips from colleagues.

6. *Learn the rules or company policies.* Recognizing that she

has to deal with the informal as well as the formal organization means *being sensitive to and aware of the customs and informal rules of conduct.* Understanding and dealing with the formal organization is sometimes easier than with the informal organization. Developing good political skills is a very important element of conscious career planning.

Questions such as "Who is really in charge?" and "Who influences the people who make big decisions?" deal with sensitive material. The woman manager who asks such questions may be perceived as aggressive. It is more tactful to ask innocent-sounding questions, such as "I am a bit confused about who is in charge of ordering a new word processor. Could you help me?"

Another trick is for the manager to balance social behavior with her work. Too much social interaction wastes her own time as well as the company's resources. Too little may keep her from getting the cooperation she needs from coworkers to accomplish her job. If she is intent on career advancement, a minimum amount of social interaction is necessary to keep her on good terms with her peers.

7. *Systematically plan her career.* Many women set their goals without consciously determining how they are going to reach them. Often they drift indecisively from job to job, or stay too long in one position. Planning helps them make better decisions at each step of their careers.

8. *Carry out her plan.* It is useless for the manager to have a plan unless she carries it out. If her plan calls for going to school, changing jobs, or requesting a raise, she should do it.

9. *Chart her progress.* Rarely will the manager's career progress as she expects it to. She should be prepared and be flexible enough to change. The entire career planning process is an ongoing, dynamic process.

Basic Everyday Tactics

Once the manager is in the midst of her career, there are many things she can do to enhance it. Career tactics become very important. To succeed in business she not only needs to be competent and to work hard, but she also needs to play sensible office politics. She should not underestimate the role that politics plays in organizational life. Some specific tactics are discussed below.

1. *Doing excellent work.* High performance and excellent work are basic foundations of a career strategy. Great political ability, in and of itself, can sometimes cause a mediocre individual to rise above others, but this doesn't happen often. As a general rule, the better the manager works, the greater her chances for success and recognition. It is only when she and her colleagues are at the same level of performance that political savvy causes her to stand out. Doing excellent work then is a prerequisite to every other tactic for advancing her career.

2. *Being visible.* In many organizations there are people who contribute a great deal, yet no one really knows about it. If the manager wants to be rewarded for her performance, she has to be sure her superiors know about it. She should remember that she is her own greatest fan! One woman manager gave the following advice: "The method of putting it down on paper . . . becoming visible . . . it's effective. People know . . . it's your idea. Instead of just calling somebody up, you send a memo . . . . Get something back."

There are several ways for a manager to advertise her actions without being viewed as a braggart or as too self-interested. Some of these ways are shown in Figure 5-3.

FIGURE 5-3

STRATEGIES FOR BEING VISIBLE

- Sending memos to her superiors when projects have been completed
- Actively soliciting feedback
- Submitting periodic progress reports

- Getting assigned to special projects and task forces
- Volunteering for different assignments
- Paying honest compliments to people

3. *Presenting the right image.* The manager wants to make

sure that as she becomes more visible she is also presenting the right image. Specific strategies for projecting the right image were discussed in Chapter 3.

4. *Helping her boss succeed.* The more the manager helps her boss, the more valuable she will be. Strategies to accomplish this include those shown in Figure 5-4.

FIGURE 5-4

STRATEGIES FOR HELPING A BOSS SUCCEED

- Displaying loyalty
- Doing good work
- Suggesting new approaches to problems
- Keeping her boss informed
- Avoiding disloyalty
- Discovering her boss's objectives

5. *Finding a sponsor.* The manager should find a high-level person to serve as an organizational ally. Strategies for finding and maintaining a sponsor, or mentor, were discussed in Chapter 4.

EEO Guidelines to Know

Since the manager essentially is responsible for her own career, she usually has to fight for herself. A basic knowledge of the law that concerns her as a woman is important.

The Civil Rights Act of 1964 provides broad overall protection for a large group of people in a variety of areas. Specifically, Title VII of this Act prohibits discrimination based on sex, race, religion, and national origin. Thus, discrimination became unlawful in the following areas: hiring and firing decisions, fringe benefits, classifying or reclassifying employees, assigning use of facilities, training and retraining, apprenticeship programs, and privileges and conditions of employment. Existing state laws which prohibited or limited the employment of women in any job were superseded by Title VII.

Certain types of employers are excluded from coverage; that is, they do not have to comply with Title VII regulations. Those organizations excluded from coverage are: all-male schools, all-female schools, or schools serving one religious group; federal and state employment systems; the District of Columbia; Indian tribes; and elected officials and their personal staffs in state and local governments.[14]

Changes Effected by EEOA. In 1972 the Equal Employment Opportunity Act amended Title VII of the Civil Rights Act of 1964. The provisions of the EEOA were more clearly defined than Title VII, and more teeth were put into their subsequent reinforcement. One change put into effect as a result of the 1972 law barred the classification or labeling of "men's jobs" and "women's jobs." It was only then that most newspapers eliminated the "Help Wanted: Female" category in their classified sections that used to list almost exclusively positions for child care, nurses, waitresses, and clerical personnel. Almost everything else could be found under "Help Wanted: Male." The 1972 law stated that punitive protective laws for women cannot be used as a reason for refusing to hire a woman.

Another change was the equalization of benefits and employment practices. Today minimum wage and overtime policies must be applied equally to both males and females. Rest periods, meal periods, and physical facilities must be provided on an equal basis for males and females.

Although an entire book could be written on the subject of comparable worth, it seems appropriate to mention this issue here. The concept underlying **comparable worth** is that jobs requiring comparable knowledge, skills, and abilities should pay at comparable levels. One view about this issue is that it is discriminatory to have a situation in which jobs of equal worth have unequal levels of compensation. It is usually the "female" jobs which have less compensation. The other view is that supply and demand, rather than discriminatory action by an employer, create the disparity in pay. This issue will be an ongoing one of great interest to females.

Finally, punitive policies concerning childbirth were eliminated by the EEOA. In the past, women had often been penalized for bearing a child by not receiving maternity leave with pay and having to return to work six months later at a lower paying and lower status job. This is no longer allowed to happen under EEOA regulations. Accrued seniority, reinstatement, and payment under existing health insurance plans and sick leave policy plans must now be applied to disability due to pregnancy, miscarriage, abortion, childbirth, and recovery from childbirth in the same manner as is done to other temporary disabilities.

What to Do if Faced with Discrimination. If the manager finds herself being discriminated against, she can take several steps:

1. *Document complaints.* She should record as precisely as possible the names, dates, times, and conversations that are relevant to her situation. She should focus her comments on *descriptions* of what happened, rather than a judgment of what has occurred. The effort to describe her situation represents a process for reporting what occurred, while judgment refers to an evaluation in terms of good and bad, right and wrong. Judgments arise out of a personal frame of reference, whereas descriptions represent neutral reporting.

2. *Don't talk about the complaint.* The manager should not speak carelessly or in anger while her complaint is being processed. It weakens her position and can lead to people perceiving her as a complainer, regardless of whether her complaint is valid or not.

3. *Confront the right parties with her problem.* Once she has sufficiently documented her case, it is time for action. She may be able to solve her problem at the lowest possible level. Some companies maintain special committees which handle grievances. Perhaps an affirmative action officer in her company is the person to see. If she cannot get satisfaction at this level, she should try another level. She should present her case clearly, articulately, and logically with her prepared documentation.

4. If she fails to achieve satisfaction within her organization and wishes to pursue the matter, she should *contact the EEOC* in her city and determine what recourse she has.

ACTION GUIDELINES

No one chapter in a book can change a woman's life, tell her how to get rid of stress entirely, or how to manage her time or career completely. However, there does seem to be a basic principle underlying much of what is known about managing stress, time, and careers. That principle is that the demands associated with valued and rewarding activities seem to be consistently less stressful and more energizing than demands associated with activities that are not personally meaningful.

The bottom line, then, appears to be not how much the manager is doing, but what she is doing and why. Women who manage their goals and priorities will have a head start on self-management. They can keep stress within optimal limits and use it to energize their efforts toward valued goals.

FOOTNOTES

1. H. Selye, *The Stress of Life* (New York: McGraw-Hill, 1976), p. 1.

2. Robert Kreitner, "Managing the Two Faces of Stress," *Arizona Business* (October, 1977), pp. 2-14.

3. Gary L. Cooper and Marilyn J. Davidson, "The High Cost of Stress on Women Managers," *Organizational Dynamics* (Spring, 1982), pp. 44-53.

4. Roger Allen, *Human Stress: Its Nature and Control* (Minneapolis: Burgess Publishing Company, 1970), p. 170.

5. Roger Allen, *Relaxation Exercises for Controlling Stress and Tension* (College Park, MD: Autumn Wind, 1979). See also B. B. Brown, *Stress and the Art of Biofeedback* (New York: Harper & Row, 1977).

6. "How to Deal with Stress on the Job," *U.S. News and World Report* (March 13, 1978), pp. 80-81.

7. Eleanor B. Schwartz and R. Alec Mackenzie, "Time Management Strategy for Women," *Management Review* (September, 1977), pp. 19-25.

8. Alan Lakein, *How to Get Control of Your Time and Your Life* (New York: Peter H. Wyden, 1973), p. 73.

9. *Ibid.*, pp. 25-27.

10. G. Baruch, R. Barnett, and C. Rivers, *Lifeprints: New Patterns of Love and Work for Today's Woman* (New York: McGraw-Hill, 1983), p. 150.

11. Douglas T. Hall, *Careers in Organizations* (Santa Monica, CA: Goodyear Publishing Co., 1976), pp. 1-5.

12. *Ibid.*, pp. 183-184.

13. Alan N. Schoonmaker, *Executive Career Strategy* (New York: American Management Associations, 1971), pp. 150-160.

14. B. Stead, *Women in Management* (Englewood Cliffs, NJ: Prentice-Hall, 1985), pp. 395-396.

Betsy Ancker-Johnson
Vice President of General Motors Corporation
in charge of Environmental Activities Staff

Responsible for the emission control and safety of General Motors products and control of pollution generated by its plants. Supervises activities related to fuel economy and international regulations. Her prior experience includes several management positions with the Boeing Company. Dr. Johnson is a member of the National Academy of Engineering; a fellow of the American Physical Society, the Institute of Electrical and Electronic Engineers, and the American Association for the Advancement of Science; and a member of the Stanford University School and Engineering Advisory Council, the Massachusetts Institute of Technology Corporation Visiting Committee, and the Board of Directors of General Mills.

Georgina J. Anderson
Account Executive
Engineering & Graphics Products
Xerox Corporation

Markets engineering equipment in half of San Diego County, helps install the equipment, and conducts training and in-house seminars at customer locations. Responsibilities include developing sales plans; maintaining industry contacts; and conducting application, productivity, and financial analyses for individual companies.

Gloria E. Bader
Management Training Specialist
Cubic Corporation

Designs and presents a variety of management courses for this aerospace/electronics corporation. Responsibilities include technical training, organization development, and internal consulting on communication and career planning for members of the organization.

Jan W. Blackford
Senior Vice President
and Regional Corporate Banking Manager
Northern Region of Wachovia Bank and Trust

Responsible for the bank's corporate relationships in Greensboro, Burlington, High Point, Asheboro, Reidsville, Thomasville, and Eden. Her prior experience includes positions in personnel and general loan administration with Wachovia. She is a member of the national Financial Accounting Standards Advisory Council, serves as chairman of the National Accounting Policies Committee of Robert Morris Associates, and serves on the advisory boards of the Payton Accounting Center at the University of Michigan and the Wake Forest University School of Accountancy.

Elaine R. Bond
Senior Vice President, Director of Corporate Systems
The Chase Manhattan Bank, N.A.

Responsible for Information Systems and Telecommunications. She is also a member of the Policy Planning Committee, a Board Member of IDC (a wholly owned subsidiary), and a member of the Corporate Responsibility Committee.

Barbara Corday
President
Columbia Pictures Television (a Unit of the Coca-Cola Company)

Responsible for every aspect of Columbia Pictures Television production, including program development for both film and tape series, movies for television, daytime programming and specials, and ongoing series production. Also serves on the Steering Committee of the Caucus of Writers, Producers, and Directors and the Steering Committee of the Hollywood Women's Coalition; leads seminars for Women in Film; and is active in the Writers Guild of America.

Roxanne J. Decyk
Senior Vice President, Corporate Relations
International Harvester Company

Responsible for corporate communications, human resources, and public affairs. Also is a member of the Economic Club of Chicago, the Chicago Network, the American Bar Association, the State Bar of Wisconsin, and the Illinois Bar Association.

Karol D. Emmerich
Vice President and Treasurer
Dayton Hudson Corporation

Responsible for management of the corporation's financing, investing, and long-range financial planning activities. Her prior experience includes National Division Account Officer for Bank of America, San Francisco. She is a member of the Financial Executives Institute, Minnesota Women's Economic Roundtable, National Association of Corporate Treasurers, and National Retail Merchants Association Treasurers Committee.

Jane Evans
President and Chief Executive Officer
Monet

Responsible for directing all aspects of the world's foremost costume jewelry manufacturer which markets products under the Monet, Yves St. Laurent (YSL), and Evoke labels. Also serves on the Board of Directors of The Equitable, Philip Morris, Catalyst, and the Fashion Institute of Technology.

Sara Finn
Director of Public Relations
University of San Diego

Has held numerous offices for the Public Relations Society of America, San Diego Press Club, Council for Advancement and Support of Education, Public Relations Club of San Diego, Public Relations Association of Southern California Colleges. Also commissioned to the International Affairs Board, City of San Diego.

Claire W. Gargalli
President
Equibank

In charge of all the day-to-day operations of Pittsburgh's third largest bank.

Judith K. Hofer
President and Chief Executive Officer
May Company

Beginning as a stock girl for May Company at age 15, she served in a variety of merchandising positions after completing her education. Prior to her present position, she was named President and Chief Executive Officer of Maier and Frank (sister-store of May Company) in 1981, making her the highest ranking woman in the retailing industry at that time. Also is a member of the Committee of 200, a select group of 200 women in business in the United States; is active in the Fashion Group; and serves on the Board of Directors of the Greyhound Corporation.

Rusty Jackson
Community Relations Field Manager
Adolph Coors Company

Responsible for designing, developing, and implementing community projects, with an emphasis on minority programs, in Washington, DC, Maryland, Virginia, and West Virginia. Her position is a part of an expansion of community involvement by Adolph Coors Company at the local level throughout the country. Her prior experience includes the positions of marketing manager with L. Sanders, Inc.; territory manager with the Lexitron Corp.; and marketing support manager for Lanier Business Products. She is a recipient of the 1984-1985 Kizzy Image and Achievement Award from the Black Women Hall of Fame Foundation.

Madelyn P. Jennings
Senior Vice President, Personnel & Administration
Gannett Co., Inc.

Directs people programs of Gannett Co., Inc., and is a member of the Gannett Management Committee. Also serves as Trustee of Russell Sage College, Member of Clarkson School of Management Business Advisory Council, Member of Board of Trustees of the Gannett Foundation, Member of Board of Directors of the American Press Institute, and Member of the Texas Women's University Foundation Board.

Judith S. Johnson
Vice President, General Counsel
Systems Management American Corporation

Directs the corporate legal department and serves as policy adviser for contract, employee, and high technology industry law. Prior to this position, she served as the Assistant Attorney General for Virginia, senior counsel for the Virginia Housing Development Authority, executive director of the Alexandria Economic Opportunity Commission, and deputy director of the Halifax County Community Action.

Paula Kelly
Director, American Language Institute
Associate Dean, College of Extended Studies
San Diego State University

Directs an ESL (English as a Second Language) program for 800 students per year from over 50 countries and manages self-support College operations functions including marketing, information systems, and fiscal accountability.

Ruby L. Larkin
Assistant Vice President and Community Relations Officer
Heritage Pullman Bank

Directs the community affairs for the bank and is responsible for planning, developing, and administering the bank's over-all community relations program. She began her career at Heritage as Community Relations Officer and also served as Personnel Manager. Other prior experience includes Office Manager of MERIT Trust Company and Administrative Secretary of The Leadership Council for Metropolitan Open Communities. She is a member of the Board of Directors of the National Association of Bank Women (South Suburban Chapter), Chicago South Chamber of Commerce, Roseland Business Development Council, and National Board of Women in Management.

M. Jacqueline McCurdy
Vice President-Industry Relations
Joseph E. Seagram & Sons, Inc.

Joining Seagram in 1976 as Associate General Counsel, she later became Vice President-Regulatory Counsel for the company until she was named to her present position. The first woman admitted to the Baltimore County Bar Association, she is also a member of the Maryland Bar Association, the American Bar Association, the Board of Associates of Towson State College, and the Board of Trustees of Hood College. Also serves as Chairman of the Board of DISCUS; trustee of BACCHUS, the college-based alcohol abuse prevention program; and member of the Committee of 200.

G. G. Michelson
Senior Vice President, External Affairs
R. H. Macy & Co., Inc.

Her prior experience includes Vice President for Employee Relations and Senior Vice President for Labor and Consumer Relations with Macy's. She serves as a Board Director of the Chubb Corporation, General Electric Company, Goodyear Tire and Rubber Company, Harper & Row, Publishers, Irving Bank Corporation and the Irving Trust Company, The Quaker Oats Company, and The Stanley Works.

Colombe M. Nicholas
President
Christian Dior-New York

Responsible for licensing the name of Christian Dior in the United States (37 licensees use the Dior trademark); finance (monitoring royalty revenues, etc.); and marketing, advertising, and overseeing the design studio.

Jenann Olsen
Director-Strategic Planning
Department of City Development
City of Milwaukee, Wisconsin

Directs short- and long-range policy planning efforts for the City of Milwaukee; presents policy recommendations to the Mayor and Common Council; coordinates policy planning activities with physical planning and with economic development, urban renewal, and housing programming; and directs city public information and promotional activities.

Angela Owens
Editorial Director
WRC-TV

Prior to her present position, she was Capitol Hill Correspondent for NBC-owned stations from 1970 to 1972 and news reporter on CHANNEL 4 NEWS from 1972 to 1984. An award winning reporter, she has won a variety of community service and journalism awards including the Capitol Press Club Award for excellence in journalism. Also is a frequent public speaker and an active volunteer in a number of local community organizations.

NBC Photo
Ray East, Photographer

122

Peggy D. Preacely
Director, Business Development
Howard Advertising Inc.

Responsible for ongoing new business development for the agency. Also has written, produced, and hosted several television programs on Black History.

Eve Rich
Chairman and Chief Executive Officer
Contempo Casuals

Under her tutelage, Contempo has grown from a California-based operation of 30 stores to a national operation of over 100 stores. Her prior experience includes Vice President and General Merchandise Manager for the Broadway Division of Carter Hawley Hale. She is a member of the Women's Trusteeship of California and the Fashion Group Foundation.

Frances E. Ruffin
Articles Editor
Black Enterprise Magazine

Responsible for developing and overseeing the assignment of all feature articles. Outlines editorial goals and the direction of each issue to the editorial staff. Approves the choice of writers and content of assignment letters. Enforces deadlines for contributors. Reads and evaluates the quality of the manuscript for clarity, focus, accuracy, color, and solid research.

Anita F. Saunders
Director of Public Affairs
WVIT-TV 30—New Britain/Hartford (a Division of Viacom Broadcasting, Inc.)

Responsible for the development of Public Affairs programming, special project programming, and documentaries. Also functions as the community liaison person for WVIT and implements agreements and projects developed in cooperation with WVIT's Minority Advisory Board and other community organizations.

Susan M. Schaffer
Vice President-Sales
Western Division
United Airlines

Responsible for $2 billion in passenger and freight sales generated from 10 Western states. Also responsible for strategic and tactical planning, direct selling, implementation of incentive programs and promotion with the travel agent, freight forwarder, and travel industry communities. Her prior experience includes Vice President—Western Region, Vice President—Inflight Services, and City Manager—Milwaukee and Greater Wisconsin Airport operations, and Inflight Services Manager—Chicago. She is a member of the Board of Directors and Vice President of Women's Forum-West.

Phyllis S. Sewell
Senior Vice President-Research & Marketing Analysis
Federated Department Stores, Inc.

Responsibilities include corporate and divisional strategic plans, studies of economic trends, studies of consumer attitudes and buying habits, studies of retail merchandising opportunities and marketing techniques, and development of effective management information systems. Also serves on Board of Directors of Lee Enterprises, Inc. and Huffy Corporation.

Pauline Allen Strayhorne
Executive Vice President, Secretary
Major Federal Savings and Loan Association

A woman of many "firsts," she was the first female elected to the board of trustees of the Savings and Loan League of Southwestern Ohio. Among other female firsts are: first black female to be elected to the Board of Trustees of the Greater Cincinnati Chamber of Commerce and first female to receive the prestigious Joseph F. Budd award from Cincinnati Chapter #84 of The Institute of Financial Education. She currently serves on the boards of the Major Federal Savings and Loan Association and the Greater Cincinnati Chamber of Commerce. She is also a member of the Cincinnati Business and Professional Women's Club, the American Society of Women Accountants, and the Ohio Valley Chapter Financial Managers for Savings Institutions.

Cheryl Nido Turpin
President and Chief Executive Officer
Weinstock's, Sacramento (a Division of Carter Hawley Hale Stores, Inc.)

Her prior experience includes the position of Executive Vice President—Apparel & Accessories for Broadway Department Stores, Los Angeles (a Division of Carter Hawley Hale Stores, Inc.); Vice President and General Merchandise Manager—Apparel & Accessories for Weinstock; and Divisional Merchandise Manager—Juniors & Coats of Gimbel's, Philadelphia.

JoAnn Zuercher
Chief, Office of Disclosure Policy
Division of Corporation Finance
U.S. Securities and Exchange Commission

Responsibilities include heading the primary rulewriting office in the Division of Corporation Finance of the SEC and supervising legal staff that draft the rules, regulations, and forms setting corporate disclosure standards.

CHAPTER 6

Developing Effective Communication Skills

<u>OUTLINE</u>

I. Need for Effective Communication

II. Special Communication Problems for Women
    A. Characteristics of Women's Speech Patterns
    B. Negative Examples in Terms of Transactional Analysis
    C. Ways to Overcome Weak Speech Patterns

III. Roadblocks to Effective Two-Way Communication
    A. Hidden Intentions
    B. Preoccupation with Tasks
    C. Emotional Involvement
    D. Distortions to Match One's Expectations
    E. Misperceptions
    F. Distrust

IV. Listening
    A. Poor Listening Habits
        1. Doing All the Talking
        2. Interrupting
        3. Avoiding Eye Contact
        4. Showing Boredom
        5. Allowing Telephone Interruptions
        6. Being Easily Distracted
    B. Active Listening

V. Ways to Overcome Sender Barriers to the Communication Process
    A. Use Redundancy
    B. Be Complete and Specific
    C. Claim the Message As Your Own
    D. Ensure That Your Messages Are Congruent
    E. Develop Credibility

VI. The Need for Adequate Feedback
    A. Types of Feedback
        1. Verbal Feedback
        2. Nonverbal Feedback
        3. Fact Feedback
        4. Feeling-Feedback
    B. Effective Use of Feedback

Action Guidelines

Communication is the activity which takes up most of a manager's time. Managers are not often alone at their desks thinking or contemplating alternatives by themselves. They spend between 50 and 90 percent of their time in interpersonal communication. Of that time, 10 percent is spent communicating with superiors, 40 percent with subordinates, and 50 percent with peers.[1] When they are not talking to their superiors, peers, or subordinates face-to-face, managers are on the telephone or writing memos and letters. It is unusual for a manager to work uninterrupted for more than a half hour during two or three days of the week. The bulk of the manager's time is spent communicating with others.

The **communication process** begins when one person sends a message—oral or written—to another with the intent of evoking a response (see Figure 6-1). *Effective communication* occurs when the receiver's interpretation of the message matches the sender's intended meaning.

FIGURE 6-1

THE COMMUNICATION PROCESS

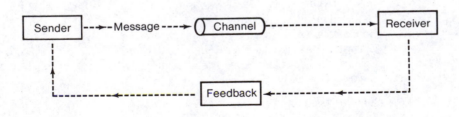

Source: Donald C. Mosley, Leon C. Megginson, and Paul H. Pietri, Jr., *Supervisory Management: The Art of Working with and through People* (Cincinnati, OH South-Western Publishing Co., 1985), p. 169.

How well do you communicate with others? If the people working for you were to rate your communication effectiveness on a scale of 1 to 10, how would you score? Have you ever had a breakdown in communication where you were misunderstood by the other person or where you misunderstood the other person's message? What were the consequences? These things happen to everyone at one time or another. Most of these barriers can be overcome, however, by mastering the skills presented in this chapter on effective communication.

NEED FOR EFFECTIVE COMMUNICATION

One can't be an effective manager without being an effective communicator. This is a truism because the very definition of managing is getting things done through other people. And if a manager can't effectively communicate what needs to be done, how can that person expect to get things accomplished? Even if the manager can accurately communicate directives, problems occur if instructions are communicated in ways that cause hard feelings or misunderstandings with other people. The result is that jobs often do not get done correctly or they may not even get done at all. This is why effective communication is a critical management skill.

Effective communication is also necessary to accomplish the management functions of *planning, organizing, staffing, directing,* and *controlling.* Plans must be communicated if they are expected to be carried out. *Organizing* involves communicating to others their responsibilities and job assignments. *Staffing* involves the solicitation of accurate information from job applicants through written, verbal, and nonverbal communication to determine effective person-job matches. *Directing* and *controlling* require interpersonal communication in order to motivate employees to strive for organizational goals and to stay on track.

Effective communication is more than simply speaking and writing well. It means choosing words carefully and knowing when to talk and when it is better to remain silent. It includes anything one does that communicates one's intentions to another person. Remember that communication is going on all of the time in many different ways through a variety of verbal and nonverbal channels.

SPECIAL COMMUNICATION PROBLEMS FOR WOMEN

Because of the complexities in the sending-receiving process, it is important to understand how women's unique speech and language patterns sometimes inhibit their effectiveness in communicating. Early social conditioning teaches women to speak like ladies. This translates into developing speech patterns which are more submissive and less incisive than men's.

Characteristics of Women's Speech Patterns

Some existing scholarly work on speech and language patterns indicates that very often fear and insecurity shape the way women talk. This is manifest in their choice of words, voice intonation, general tone of hesitancy, and their high pitch which is often interpreted as an appeal for help. The following characteristics have been found to be generally consistent in women's speech.[2] It is important to correct them because they can detract from a woman's influence and credibility.

1. The use of **empty adjectives** that connote little meaning and have a "fluffing" effect. For example, "marvelous," "divine," "terrible," etc. are empty adjectives. People whose speech is filled with empty adjectives are usually not taken very seriously.

2. The use of **tag questions** after a declarative statement which automatically defer and pass the ball to the other court. For example, "It's really time for a break now, right?" By itself, the statement shows confidence and conviction. By adding the tag question, however, the speaker gives the impression of being unsure of herself. Tag questions avoid conflicts but they also surrender the speaker's decision-making power.

3. The **questioning intonation** at the end of a statement which neutralizes or eliminates the intended assertiveness of the statement. This has the same effect as a tag question.

4. The use of **hedging or modifying phrases** which detract from the impact of a statement. Phrases such as "sort of" and "I guess" give speech a tentative and uncommitted quality.

5. The use of **hypercorrect or excessively polite speech** which may be misinterpreted. Some examples are not using contractions (i.e., don't) or being overly cautious about using slang or swearing. Instead of building respect and status, hypercorrect or excessively polite speech can give the speaker an uptight image which is often described behind her back with the very words or adjectives that she so carefully avoids. This can also detract from communication effectiveness because the speaker concentrates so much on the correctness of speech that the intended meaning is not conveyed.

6. The use of **disclaimers** which preface an opinion to protect the speaker from losing face if she's wrong. For example, "I'm probably misinformed, but" or "I'm not 100 percent sure, but." Disclaimers decrease the level of the speaker's influence. In fact, disclaimers almost invite listeners to disagree and try to prove that the speaker is wrong.

7. The use of **fillers** such as "um" and "uh" signal uncertainty and lack of preparation. Fillers also open the door for interruption and allow others to take away the speaker's right to speak.

8. The use of **apologies** that rob the speaker's requests or declarations of their focus and authority is seen in statements such as, "I really hate to bother you now because I know that you are really busy, but I'd like to ask you to take a minute and edit this memo for me." Apologies clutter and lengthen a request. They detract from the speaker's stature and influence. Compare the above lengthy request with "Take a minute to edit this memo."

9. The *overuse* of the word *try* which signals weakness. For example, "I'll try to get the report done on time." The word *try* in this response makes the manager sound frail and incompetent. Compare this response with "You've got it!"

Most of the above examples describe women's tendency to back off from strong assertions. This type of speech pattern may reflect perceived power differences which already exist or, even more important, they may actually help to create them.[3]

Finally, women have been found to use *smiles and nods* more than men in business conversations.[4] In studies of low- and high-status language behaviors, women were perceived to have greater power when they smiled less and held their heads relatively still.

The reasons for these behaviors are probably partially based on past cultural conditioning which inhibits many women from stating directly what they want or from selling what they believe in if it means overriding the opinions of others. The temptation is there to revert to the ingenue role, the seductive role, or the little girl role which worked so well as a child. A simple glance or gesture is often all that is required to do it.[5]

Negative Examples in Terms of Transactional Analysis

The goal of effective communication, in terms of **transactional analysis** (TA), is an adult-adult, problem-solving type of interaction.[6] When women revert to the more passive roles just described in the previous section, the father-daughter, mother-son, or mother-daughter relationship develops. Take the following negative examples:[7]

- ◆ A woman manager defers to a male peer on a policymaking issue (father-daughter pattern).
- ◆ Although a male manager may be angry at a female manager for an error she made, he still acts in such a way as to protect her (father-daughter pattern).
- ◆ Male and female managers use sex to play out power and control issues (father-daughter or mother-son patterns).
- ◆ Men use female managers as mothers by telling them about personal problems, but not treating them as real colleagues with whom they also

share professional problems and perform tasks (mother-son pattern).

♦ In emotional situations, a male manager may defer to a female manager if he needs sympathy or support (mother-son pattern). For example, a male manager might step aside after a confrontation with a secretary who bursts into tears and call for a female manager to comfort her.

♦ Finally, there might be instances of women managers not sharing their competence with each other, but instead behaving in a negative mother-daughter pattern.

Ways to Overcome Weak Speech Patterns

In all of the above examples, women managers allow themselves to lose communication effectiveness by reverting to the role of a parent or a child. To be more effective in communicating, women managers with these tendencies should combine the adult problem-solving mode with whatever strengths they may have as nurturing parents and their creativity as spontaneous children. By acting as adults, they can avoid communication problems and be able to love, assert, express anger and fear, be caring, and solve problems with an image of strength and confidence. The following guidelines may help:[8]

1. It may help the manager to *monitor her speech*. She should tape-record and listen to her own conversations for a few days to detect undesirable speech patterns. She should plan how she might phrase her statements more powerfully and practice doing so in role-playing sessions by herself or with an understanding friend.

2. The manager should avoid apologizing for her thoughts and feelings. She should *talk in terms of herself* and begin by using "I, my, I want, I need," etc. These are clear statements of what she wants, feels, or thinks. They connote power and decisiveness.

3. The manager should *talk in specifics, not generalities*. It is not always wise or necessary to use euphemisms to be tactful or polite. Often it's better to state directly what's on one's mind. "We aren't getting it together" is not nearly as effective as "Your late report cost us that contract."

ROADBLOCKS TO EFFECTIVE TWO-WAY COMMUNICATION

The consequences of ineffective communication—for both women and men—are varied. Ineffective communication can have the far-reaching effects of annoying a superior, causing someone to be stereotyped, promoting defensive and hostile attitudes, or producing negative evaluations which can result in reprimand or even dismissal. But perhaps the most basic and recurring consequence of poor communication is that the receiver of a message interprets it differently from the way the sender intended.

In addition to the special female communication problems described in the previous section, there are a multitude of difficulties existing within the communication process for both males and females. Some of the more common roadblocks to effective two-way communication are described below.

Hidden Intentions

The sender's intentions are private and exist only in the mind. These intentions are not always made clear, especially if they concern feelings of liking or disliking. Such feelings are usually not directly stated but implied either verbally or nonverbally. The old cliché "Wouldn't you like to come up and see my etchings?" is a good example of this. For clear communication to occur, the receiver in a situation like this must accurately decipher the true intentions behind the stated message.

The manager's use of hypercorrect speech, tag questions, and questioning intonation are good examples of acting on hidden intentions. In general, however, women have less difficulty with this roadblock than men because they are usually more open and willing to reveal their attitudes, beliefs, and concerns than males.[9] Women managers are known to be better self-disclosers than their male counterparts who more often portray the stereotypical "strong, silent type."

Preoccupation with Tasks

Oftentimes managers are so preoccupied with tasks that, when someone approaches to talk with them, they are not able to detach themselves from the tasks to listen effectively. When this happens, not only do they fail to receive the message the sender intends, but they also may communicate a feeling of not caring. This causes the sender to have negative feelings and makes future communication even more difficult.

Preoccupation is probably a greater problem for male managers, who are more task-oriented than female managers.[10] Female managers are more socially oriented and are usually more willing to take a break from tasks to help or affiliate with others.

Emotional Involvement

When managers become emotionally involved in a topic under discussion, they often are so interested in what they are saying that they listen to the other person only to find an opening to say what's on their mind. Consequently, they may miss entirely the meaning of the other person's message in their haste to get their point across.

Although females are generally seen as more emotional than males, female managers have been found to be more receptive than male managers when communicating with subordinates.[11] Males, who are more concerned with dominance and contentiousness, have more difficulty paying attention and listening.

Distortions to Match One's Expectations

There are times when managers listen only to evaluate and to make judgments about a subordinate. The subordinate usually is aware of this evaluation because of a manager's reactions. Consequently, the subordinate becomes guarded and defensive. Very often the result is that the subordinate tends to cover up inadequacies to insure a positive reaction from the manager rather than communicate the real concerns that caused the communication to be initiated in the first place.

Women managers must be especially aware of this evaluation procedure when they are communicating with male superiors, peers, and subordinates. This is especially crucial during the female manager's initial stages on a new job, when males typically seek to test her competencies and ability to "act like a manager." Female managers should be particularly sensitive to the use of empty adjectives, tag questions, and hedging phrases which may be interpreted by males as signs of insecurity or dependence. Both of these signs are seen as typical female handicaps and evidence of incompetence in managerial positions.

Misperceptions

It is much easier to hear the words being spoken than to understand their intended meaning. For example, the words "it's a nice day" might be intended to be taken literally; but the speaker also might have intended to use them for the purpose of changing the subject to something more relevant. A misperception on the part of the receiver of such a message—which could cause the receiver to take these words literally and proceed as if the sender were really interested in the weather—would only continue the comedy of errors.

It is very important for female managers to use their sensitivity and ability to "read" the underlying intentions of their male counterparts before accepting at face value all that is said by them. Female managers' strengths in sensitivity, affiliation, and promoting positive relations can actually get in the way of effective communication if they don't take into consideration the subtle, subsurface gamesmanship which is typical of male interactions from adolescence through adulthood. Males tend to compete and challenge, often through more subtle innuendos. However, this doesn't mean that males are always manipulative and applying a hidden agenda when dealing with others. Such gamesmanship usually occurs when males are interacting among themselves in clearly defined competitive situations. If female managers do not make distinctions in accordance with specific situations, inappropriate distrust can develop.[12]

Distrust

Lack of trust causes a decrease in the amount of information shared and an increase in suspiciousness regarding the validity of the information. The restricted communication that results from distrust often originates from many of the problem areas previously discussed. A fair degree of paranoia is probably functional for new women managers because, initially, males do attempt to test out their competence and ability to meet social expectations. However, after the women managers have proven themselves and have been accepted, they need only to exercise normal discretion.

Males may be confused by their own emotional ambiguity when working with females in positions of authority. On the other hand, most women have a plus in the area of perceived trustworthiness because of their relatively higher degree of self-disclosure, openness, and sociability. Women must be careful to disclose only appropriate information about themselves and not to be too open, however. Excesses in these behaviors can promote the feminine stereotype and "mother role." **Strategic openness**—disclosure when appropriate—is a key consideration.

Although the above is a formidable list of barriers to communication—and most people have experienced one or more of these on a frequent basis—there are things managers can do to overcome these barriers. *Active* listening on the part of the receiver is so important that the next section is devoted entirely to this topic. The remainder of the chapter will be concerned with other strategies for overcoming these barriers.

LISTENING

Listening is not the same as hearing. People usually hear the entire message, but too often its meaning is lost or distorted. **Listening** is an intellectual and emotional process in which one integrates physical, emotional, and intellectual inputs in search of meaning. In order to be good listeners, managers should be objective. This requires a conscious attempt to understand the speaker without letting personal opinions influence the content of the speaker's message. Managers should concentrate on understanding what the speaker wants to communicate, not what they want to hear.

The normal untrained listener is likely to understand and retain only about 50 percent of a conversation. This relatively low percentage drops to an even less impressive 25 percent retention rate 48 hours later.[13] This means that recall from memory of a particular conversation which took place more than a couple of days before will always be incomplete and usually inaccurate. This is one reason why people often disagree about what has been discussed!

Listening to employees is one of the most valuable and effective tools for helping those employees feel understood and accepted by their manager. It helps to accurately determine the employees' problems and goals and to understand how the employees really feel about them. The solutions that managers propose will be more meaningful and relevant and they will at least be tried by the employees. In addition, the employees will usually reciprocate by really listening to the managers when they speak.

Female managers are probably better listeners than male managers. Females typically show more concern, encouragement, attentiveness, and receptiveness than males.[14] Not all female managers are equally good listeners, however. And even when they are listening effectively, they need to demonstrate this to others by communicating their attentiveness through alert eye contact and body posture.

Poor Listening Habits

There are a number of poor listening habits that often inhibit a manager's ability to listen effectively. While reading about the habits described below, the woman manager should try to determine objectively if she is guilty of any of them. If so, she will know where to begin her program for improvement in the art of listening.

Doing All the Talking. Many managers, especially male managers, believe that speech is power. They monopolize the conversation by doing all the talking. They tell their employees what their problems are and how to solve them.

Interrupting. How would a manager feel if somebody finished her statements or told her, "I know what you mean," before she has even finished her message? A manager should allow her employee the courtesy of completing his or her train of thought, which might even be very different from what she assumed.

Avoiding Eye Contact. Although people listen with their ears, they judge whether the receiver of a message is listening by looking at his or her eyes. Maintaining a gentle, intermittent eye contact is one of the most integral skills of an effective listener.

Showing Boredom. Managers sometimes communicate boredom while someone is talking by toying with a pencil, fixing their hair, doodling, shuffling through papers, wiping glasses, or playing with objects. Some classic examples of showing boredom occur when a manager frequently looks at her watch while the other person is speaking, or does not stop what she is doing as the other person talks. Managers can also show boredom when they act rushed and make comments about their busy day when a subordinate is trying to explain a problem.

Allowing Telephone Interruptions. Managers frequently ignore their employees by taking incoming phone calls or by making outgoing phone calls while employees are in the office to have a serious conversation. When a manager interrupts the employee because of an incoming phone call, it makes the employee feel unimportant. The manager should hold all incoming calls while employees are in the office, or at least take the phone off the hook.

Being Easily Distracted. Employees resent managers who are too easily distracted from the conversation by external noise, passersby, and employee statements that remind them of prior experiences they've had or have heard of. For example, they resent the manager who always looks out the window to see if anything more interesting is happening outside the office. They resent the manager who consistently interrupts the conversation by saying, "That reminds me of . . ."

Active Listening

The active listener is skilled at sensing, attending, and responding.[15] **Sensing** is the ability to recognize the silent messages (i.e., vocal intonation, body language, facial expressions) that the speaker is sending. **Attending** refers to the verbal, vocal, and visual messages that the active listener sends to the speaker. This includes appropriate eye contact, open body language, affirmative head nods, and appropriate facial and verbal expressions. **Responding** refers to the active listener's giving feedback on the accuracy of the speaker's message and feelings, keeping the speaker talking, gathering more information, making the speaker feel understood, and getting the speaker to better understand the problems or concerns being discussed.

Active listening takes great concentration and attention. But unless a manager practices active listening in managerial relationships, that manager doesn't know what it means to be a "good communicator."

WAYS TO OVERCOME SENDER BARRIERS TO THE COMMUNICATION PROCESS

From the sender's viewpoint, perhaps the most crucial difficulty in effective communication is getting the receiver of a message to understand it in the way the sender intended. To increase the likelihood of a message being correctly understood, managers can employ the strategies explained below.

Use Redundancy

Redundancy means using more than one channel of communication. For example, when speaking with her employees, the manager might use the appropriate facial and body gestures, diagram what she is talking about, and summarize her message on a piece of paper. This ensures that the receiver has the opportunity to receive her message through more than one of the senses.

Be Complete and Specific

Another way to ensure that a message will be understood is to make it *complete* and *specific*. Here it is important to give all of the background information necessary for the receiver to understand the manager's frame of reference and intentions. Then the manager should refer to concrete deadlines and examples so as to leave no room for misunderstanding by the receiver.

Claim the Message as Your Own

It's also important for the manager to claim the message as her *own*. To do this, she should use personal pronouns such as "I" and "mine." This means that she is taking responsibility for her ideas and for the feelings that she expresses. This type of mindset also helps counter tendencies to abdicate responsibility through tag questions and hedging phrases.

Ensure That Your Messages Are Congruent

The manager should make sure that her verbal and nonverbal messages are *congruent*. If she tells her employees that she is there to help them but, when they come in with problems, she acts in a frustrated and condescending way, she is really communicating something which is quite a bit different from her original message.

Develop Credibility

A manager's **credibility** as a sender is probably the single most important element in effective interpersonal communication.

A sender's credibility is evidenced by the belief on the part of the receiver that the sender is trustworthy. Several factors that can affect sender credibility are described below.

1. *Expertness.* It is important that the sender of a message be perceived by the receiver as an expert on the topic under discussion. A subordinate is much more apt to listen to the manager's opinions on how to complete a work-related project than on how the subordinate should run his or her life. Although formal education and degrees help managers to be perceived as experts, their track records and on-the-job experience are the key indicators. Women managers' credibility is enhanced significantly once they "prove" themselves on the job.

2. *Motives.* The receiver of a message is also concerned with the sender's motives. Does the subordinate perceive a manager's motives for sending a message as selfish or as helpful to the subordinate? Managers should be open about their motives because it is very difficult to hide them. Owning up to motives tactfully at the very beginning will allow the employees to see the manager's intentions for what they are in a more positive way. It will also save the employees unnecessary anxiety and waste of energy that otherwise would be spent in trying to discover what the manager's underlying motives really are.

3. *Reliability.* Managers are an important information source to their subordinates. Reliability as an information source is evidenced by the employees' perceptions that a manager is dependable, predictable, and consistent. Being up to date on new developments affecting the work group's productivity also increases perceptions of the manager's expertise and competence. Some important questions that managers should ask themselves in this regard are: Am I always prepared to provide the information subordinates require? Will I be consistent in my applications of criteria for success? Can all subordinates count on me to treat them equally?

4. *Warmth and friendliness.* A manager who is warm and friendly is more apt to be helpful than one who walks

around in a hostile manner with a chip on her shoulder. Whom would you approach with work or personal problems? With whom would you be more likely to communicate about your uncertainties or hesitancies in implementing a new procedure for solving a difficult problem?

This factor in establishing credibility is especially important for women managers because it is expected more of them than of males. Baird and Bradley's study of 150 people in three large organizations showed that female managers exceeded males in promoting positive relations and showing concern for subordinates.[16] If subordinates did not perceive their female supervisors as being warm and friendly, the subordinates rated them lower in supervisory effectiveness. This was not the case for male supervisors, who were expected to be more task-oriented and quick to challenge but not necessarily warm and friendly.

5. *Dynamism.* A dynamic manager who is assertive, emphatic, and forceful sends more credible messages than one who appears passive, withdrawn, and unsure of herself. If a manager expects people to pay attention and act on her messages, she needs to put the necessary energy into asserting herself and making sure that the importance of her request is understood.

6. *Opinions of others.* If friends or other staff members tell the receiver that the sender is trustworthy, the receiver will tend to believe it. If, on the other hand, a sender's image has been tarnished through a negative reputation, the opposite will probably occur. This is the phenomenon known as the **self-fulfilling prophecy**: expectations are usually acted upon and confirmed.

In summary, there isn't any evidence indicating that any one of the above factors in sender credibility is more important than the others. A high-credibility sender scores high on all of these factors, but a low-credibility sender only has to be low on any one of them. Therefore, a manager needs to increase emphasis on all of these factors. Otherwise, a receiver is likely to discount her message and she won't be able to communicate effectively.

THE NEED FOR ADEQUATE FEEDBACK

One of the best ways to insure a receiver's accuracy in understanding the sender's message is to provide adequate feedback. **Feedback** is the process of the receiver telling the sender exactly what the receiver has heard and what the receiver thinks the meaning of the message is. In the feedback process the sender perceives how the message was being decoded and received. The response the receiver makes can then allow the sender to modify the original message if necessary.

If the manager is not able to obtain feedback on how her message is being decoded, inaccuracies may occur that may never be corrected. The main way to correct inaccuracies in communication is through the process of feedback. For example, when a boss says, "Call me later and we'll discuss it," does the boss mean 15 minutes from now, one hour from now, tomorrow, or next week? When a memo states, "Men cannot wear long hair," does "long hair" mean hair covering the ears, to the collar, past the collar, or to the waist? These statements, like millions of others, can have unlimited meanings. They create a high probability of misunderstanding in communication. Unless statements such as these are clarified, there is a great likelihood that they will be misunderstood. The directions and instructions will not be followed as intended, and the relationship between both parties may be strained. Through the application of feedback skills, these highly ambiguous statements can be transformed into very specific effective communication.

Like listening, the use of feedback in the process of communication is very often taken for granted. Feedback may, however, actually be the most important aspect of interpersonal communication. If there were no feedback, how would each person "really" know what the other person was talking about? In conversations with employees, fellow managers, and superiors, how often have you felt like saying to them, "I know you think you understand what I said, but I'm not so sure that what you heard is what I meant." The effective use of feedback skills helps reduce the probability of this type of misunderstanding and misinterpretation.

Types of Feedback

Feedback can be given verbally or nonverbally. Its purpose can be to verify facts or feelings.

Verbal Feedback. Verbal feedback is the type that people are most frequently aware of and that they use most often. The manager can use verbal feedback to ask for a clarification of her employee's message, or she can use it to give positive and/or negative strokes.

By asking employees simple questions, the manager can determine whether she should keep proceeding in the same direction or modify her approach. For example, a question such as, "Shall we explore that issue some more?" allows her to determine her employee's interest level in the current topic of conversation rather than capriciously cutting the topic too short or dragging on too long. Another example of a feedback question is, "Would you like me to get right into the details of this job, or do you have some other questions that you'd like to ask me first?" This question allows her to determine the employee's present state of mind and level of receptivity to the information she is about to give. Without asking this question, she might continue with more details of the job when the employee has a number of questions he or she would have liked to ask first.

Verbal feedback can also be used by managers to give positive and negative strokes to their employees. Simple statements such as, "You did a really good job," "I really trust you," and "Keep up the good work," show the employees specifically that the manager recognizes and appreciates what they are doing. This type of feedback prompts them to continue to perform in a positive manner.

When an employee's behavior gets out of line, negative feedback can be given to correct the deviation. It is often destructive just to ignore an employee's deviant personal or work behavior. Silence may be construed by the employee as tacit approval. Comments to the employee such as, "Sarah told me she is afraid to be near you because you always come on too strong with her," or "You didn't complete the job by the 10:00 a.m. deadline" provide the employee with the type of verbal feedback required to correct the deviant behavior.

During a conversation, managers need to make sure that they understand what the employees are communicating to them. Managers can encourage the employees to do the same with them. If the employees do not provide feedback about a manager's message, it can be beneficial for the manager to ask each of them to restate his or her interpretation of the message.

Most clarifying feedback typically begins and ends with statements such as those shown in Figure 6-2.

FIGURE 6-2

CLARIFYING FEEDBACK STATEMENTS

Begin with:

- "Let me be sure I understand what you have said."
- "Let me see if I can summarize the key points we've discussed."
- "I hear you saying . . . "
- "I think I hear you saying that your central concern is . . . "
- "As I understand it, your major objectives are . . . "

End with:

- "Did I understand you properly?"
- "Did I hear you correctly?"
- "Was I on target with what you meant?"
- "Were those your major concerns?"
- "Can you add anything to my summary?"

Nonverbal Feedback. The body, eyes, face, and posture can communicate a variety of positive or negative attitudes, feelings, or opinions. Continuous nonverbal feedback occurs consciously and unconsciously in communication between supervisors and subordinates. Perceptive communicators utilize nonverbal feedback from their receivers to structure the content and direction of their own messages.

The amount of nonverbal feedback the manager receives is not as important as how she interprets it and reacts to it. When she is losing the employee's interest, she can react to that nonverbal feedback by changing her pace, topic, or tone of voice.

It is also easy to send **mixed signals** to employees. This means that while the manager is saying one thing, she is communicating something totally different through her body language. These mixed signals force the employee to choose between the verbal and the visual aspects of her message. Most often, they choose the nonverbal aspect of the message.

Mixed signals also create a level of tension and distrust. Rightly or wrongly, receivers feel that senders are purposely hiding something from them or are being less than candid. Tones of hesitancy and tentative speech styles like "sort of" are typical examples of nonverbal feedback sent by female managers through mixed signals.

Fact Feedback. Fact-finding questions are meant to elicit specific data and information. If the facts are worth soliciting from the employees, they are certainly worth being heard accurately.

Fact feedback is also important when managers are relating important factual information to employees. When they are depending on the manager's facts, it is critically important to give employees exact information.

Fact feedback is useful when managers want clarification, agreement, or correction. It also is useful in the translation of messages and in the interpretation of words and phrases. The following messages contain words or phrases that are quite unclear. They are perfect candidates for fact-feedback statements.

- ◆ "Due to recent layoffs, all employees are expected to work harder from now on."
- ◆ "Don't spend too much time on that job."
- ◆ "We will be visiting Philadelphia and New York City. We expect to open our first unit there."

When there is a chance for something to be misunderstood, it will be misunderstood. Fact-feedback can be used to make messages clear.

Feeling-Feedback. The best **feeling-feedback** is two-directional. The receiver makes a concerted effort to really understand the feelings, emotions, and attitudes that underlie the sender's message. In addition, the receiver projects feeling-feedback to the sender to let the sender know that the messages have gotten through—at the gut level. Whereas fact feedback is a meeting of the minds, feeling-feedback is a meeting of the hearts.

Feeling-feedback is the effective use of **empathy**, which is putting oneself into another's shoes so that one can see things from the other person's point of view. When the manager can really feel the employees' true feelings and understand where they are coming from and, at the same time, project this emotional awareness to them, this serves to reinforce rapport, to lower interpersonal tension, and to significantly increase trust.

Effective Use of Feedback

The manager should take a few moments to recall the times where she could have smoothed over some communication problems simply by using some of the forms of feedback discussed above. Effective communication between two people is never easy. The manager really has the primary responsibility to make it work. The following guidelines are designed to facilitate the use of feedback skills which will enhance communication effectiveness.

1. *Give and get definitions.* The interpretations of words or phrases may vary from males to females, supervisors to subordinates, or from one group to another. When people believe or assume that words have one and only one meaning, it causes situations in which they assume or pretend that they understand others but they really do not. This eventually leads to subsequent misunderstandings, breakdowns in communication, and decreased trust. To avoid such situations, the manager should give and get definitions of dubious words or phrases. For example, instead of assuming that a subordinate knows what the manager means when she tells him or her to "Take your time and do it right," the manager should define exactly what she means by saying, "Take another day to make sure the project meets the exact specifications." Otherwise, the manager may end up not hearing from the subordinate for a month because he or she interpreted "take your time" as an indefinite period.

2. *Don't make assumptions.* Making assumptions invariably causes misunderstanding. During interpersonal communication, it is highly dangerous for a manager to make the assumption that the other person either thinks or feels as she does at that moment. The other person may have a frame of reference that is totally different from that of the manager's. The manager should not assume that she and the other person are talking about the same thing. She shouldn't assume that the words and phrases that they are both using are automatically being understood. For example, a manager who assumes that an employee is as concerned about meeting a deadline as the manager is, and will work late to do it, can be in for some frustration and disappointment.

   The classic phrase uttered by people who make assumptions is "I know exactly what you mean." Many people use that statement without ever using feedback skills to determine exactly what the other person means. By using more feedback and making fewer assumptions, the accuracy of interpersonal communication can be greatly enhanced.

3. *Ask questions.* A good rule of thumb is, "when in doubt, check it out." One of the best ways to "check it out" is through the effective use of questioning skills. The manager should ask clarifying questions, key questions, fact-finding questions, and feeling-finding questions freely during conversation to get feedback.

4. *Simplify language.* The manager should abstain from using words that can be easily misinterpreted or mistranslated, especially technical terms and company jargon. Some terms which are familiar to the manager may be totally foreign to the people with whom she talks. It is a good idea for her to simplify her language and her technical terms so that every one of the employees can understand her and feed back to her exactly what she meant.

5. *Keep tuned in.* In a conversation, the manager should observe the other person, be sensitive to the feelings the person is experiencing during their interaction, and respond to those feelings appropriately. The receiver's nonverbal feedback may mean that the sender should change his or her approach or message accordingly.

6. *Give feedback on the behavior, not the person.* This relates to the manager's appropriate use of positive and negative feedback or "strokes" with employees. When they do something especially well, the manager should give them positive feedback and relate it specifically to the action or behavior that was performed. When they do something especially bad, she should give them negative feedback directed specifically toward the action or behavior that needs to be corrected.

It is not appropriate under any circumstance to criticize an employee personally because of an inappropriate action. This is not only degrading but also counterproductive. Many ineffective managers, upon learning that one of their employees did something wrong, criticize that employee personally by saying, "You're an idiot, that was really stupid," or "You can't do anything right, can you?" These statements constitute inappropriate feedback. On the other hand, the employees may believe these statements, and they can become a negative self-fulfilling prophecy. In any case, how can a manager expect an employee to improve performance on a particular task or behavior unless the employee knows specifically which behavior or action must be corrected?

7. *Know when to withhold feedback.* There are times when it's best not to give feedback. Sometimes the manager should bite her tongue and restrain her body language and facial expressions in certain situations. Examples are situations where the employee cannot effectively cope with any more negative feedback, or the feedback concerns something the employee cannot do anything about anyway.

ACTION GUIDELINES

One can't be an effective manager without being an effective communicator. Getting things accomplished through the efforts of other people requires that they understand exactly what needs to be done, when, and how. This won't happen without accurate and effective communication. The following are some guidelines which can enhance the manager's effectiveness in communicating.

1. The manager should be aware of the traditional female communication problems that she may suffer from. These include the use of "empty adjectives," "tag questions," "hedging phrases," and excessively polite speech. Monitoring her speech through a tape recorder may help her detect some of these power-robbing flaws. She should avoid communication idiosyncrasies through the use of an adult-adult, problem-solving type of interaction.

2. The manager should be aware of common roadblocks to communication like hidden intentions, preoccupation, emotional involvement, distortions to match expectations, misperceptions, and distrust. The techniques discussed in this chapter can be used to get around these roadblocks.

3. The manager should avoid poor listening habits like doing all the talking, interrupting, lack of eye contact, showing boredom, allowing telephone interruptions, and being easily distracted. She should enhance her active listening skills through sensing, attending, responding, and empathizing.

4. The manager should overcome barriers to effective communication by using redundancy, being complete and specific, claiming the message as her own, ensuring that her messages are congruent, and developing her credibility.

5. The manager should use feedback effectively by giving or getting definitions, not making assumptions, asking questions, simplifying language, being aware of the speaker's feelings, giving feedback on the behavior and not the person, and knowing when to withhold feedback.

FOOTNOTES

1. A. G. Sargent, "The Androgynous Blend: Best of Both Worlds," *Management Review* (October, 1978), pp. 60-65.

2. R. Lakoff, "Language and Women's Place," *Language in Society*, 2 (1973), pp. 45-79.

3. M. B. Parlee, "Conversational Politics," *Psychology Today* (May, 1979), pp. 28-38.

4. M. R. Key, *Male/Female Language* (Netuchen, NJ: Scarecrow Press, 1981).

5. G. Sassen, "Success Anxiety in Women: A Constructivist Interpretation of Its Source and Its Significance," *Harvard Educational Review*, Vol. 50, No. 1 (February, 1980), pp. 21-22.

6. For a detailed discussion of transactional analysis, a technique developed originally by Eric Berne, see his *Transactional Analysis in Psychotherapy* (New York: Grove Press, 1961).

7. A. G. Sargent, *op. cit.*, p. 65.

8. S. H. Vogler, "Talking Tough—It's Not What You Say, But How You Say It," *Working Women*, 8 (April, 1983), pp. 34-35.

9. J. E. Baird, Jr., and P. H. Bradley, "Styles of Management and Communication: A Comparative Study of Men and Women," *Communication Monographs*, 46 (June, 1979), pp. 101-111.

10. E. F. Borgetta and J. Stimson, "Sex Differences in Interaction Characteristics," *Journal of Social Psychology*, 60 (1963), pp. 89-100.

11. Baird and Bradley, *op. cit.*, pp. 101-111.

12. J. Pfeiffer, "Girl Talk-Boy Talk," *Science*, 85 (January-February, 1985), pp. 58-63.

13. R. G. Nichols, "Listening Is a Ten-Part Skill," *Nation's Business*, Vol. 45 (July, 1957), pp. 56-60.

14. Baird and Bradley, *op. cit.*, pp. 101-111.

15. P. L. Hunsaker and A. J. Alessandra, *The Art of Managing People* (Englewood Cliffs, NJ: Prentice-Hall, 1980), pp. 130-131.

16. Baird and Bradley, *op. cit.*, pp. 101-111.

CHAPTER 7

Handling Power and Politics

OUTLINE

I. Traditional Power Failures of Women Managers

II. Sources of Power for Women Managers
   A. Legitimate Power
   B. Reward Power
   C. Coercive Power
   D. Referent Power
   E. Expert Power
   F. Information Power

III. Power and the Woman Manager's Career
   A. Using Feminine Characteristics to Advantage
   B. Adopting a Masculine Style of Behavior
   C. Seeking Entry into "Old Boys' Network"

IV. Strategies for Enhancing Interpersonal Power
   A. Be Assertive
   B. Be Courteous
   C. Direct Your Thinking
   D. Neutralize Resistance
   E. Inoculate the Key Decision Makers
   F. Use the Media
   G. Build Support Groups
   H. Gatekeep
   I. Hold Out
   J. Go Around
   K. Threaten to Resign

V. Sex as a Power Tactic
   A. Flirtation
   B. Dating
   C. Flings
   D. Affairs

Action Guidelines

When women move into managerial roles in organizations, the exercise of power and authority is required. One extreme view is that a woman manager can easily accept these new role requirements and exercise new behaviors necessary to deal with power and politics. In quoting Michael Korda's article on "Sexual Office Politics" in an issue of *Playboy* magazine, Horn and Horn share his conviction that women who gain power can be tougher infighters than the men they deal with. The willingness of women to use their sexuality to get what they want can be part of their strength. A woman who knows her business and has a position of power can refuse to accept sexual put-downs and even chop a man off at the knees if the situation warrants it.[1]

One woman executive said, "The competition is going to get a lot hotter . . . Women have always used sex as a substitute for power, a way of fighting back; and men have thought of sex as a way of keeping women in their place." This executive sees sex between equals as a revolutionary idea, not only in bed, but also in office politics.[2]

The other extreme, often voiced by new women managers, is that they do not want to get involved in organizational politics at all. They just want to do their job and stay out of "all that other stuff." Unfortunately, this is not possible. Managers are involved in politics as soon as they start to work for an organization. Because people in the organization are human, they have different backgrounds, values, aspirations, and objectives. These elements all enter into the job and affect the performance and feelings of everyone in the organization.

Office politics is getting all the different human elements to work for a person rather than against him or her. Although it is very important for the woman manager to do her job effectively, it is also important that others like and respect her, especially those whose opinions count in rewarding her managerial competence.

Understanding the uses of power is integral to understanding organizational politics. Power influences a manager's effectiveness—whether the manager is dealing with one or two people or with an entire organization. Many women, however, prefer not to think of their jobs in terms of power. Ask them how power oriented they are and they'll reply modestly, "Not at all." This reply is probably based more on early cultural conditioning than on true feelings.

Everyone has attitudes toward power, and it is the exercise of power that determines how well individuals perform in their roles.

TRADITIONAL POWER FAILURES OF WOMEN MANAGERS[3]

Most businesswomen, even those in management, usually find themselves occupying the more routine and low-profile types of jobs. Examples are *staff positions* where they serve in support capacities to line managers and have no direct responsibilities of their own, or in supervisory jobs managing periphery activities which do not allow them to develop credibility or to influence subordinates. Such jobs have few favors to trade and therefore keep women managers out of the mainstream of organizational politics. Their corresponding lack of clout and exclusion from information and support networks make women in these positions structurally powerless.

Another problem stems from good intentions on the part of male superiors who actually are trying to give their female subordinates every chance to succeed. Well-intentioned male managers who hold traditional stereotypes of women may try to protect female managers from the organizational jungle they "are not too equipped to survive in." *Overprotecting* female managers by putting them in "safe" jobs does more harm than good. First, it does not provide a chance for female managers to prove themselves; and, second, not giving them higher-risk projects keeps their visibility low.

Overprotectiveness can also occur in situations where male superiors are fearful of being associated with a female subordinate should she fail in a difficult assignment. This situation often develops where chauvinistic attitudes prevail in the overall organization. Even if the male superior has had overwhelmingly positive work experiences with his female subordinate, he may feel that assigning her more challenging projects involves a *personal risk*. He knows that other managers are not as accepting of women as he is; and if she doesn't succeed, he has stuck his neck out and his reputation and future judgment will be on the line.

An even stronger blow to a female manager's power potential is dealt in situations where her superior shows obvious signs of lack of support and confidence in her. *Lack of support* is manifest in behaviors such as allowing the female manager to be bypassed easily when those reporting to her disagree with her decisions, or when her superior is always eager to listen to criticism about her and is overly concerned with any negative comment about her. This type of behavior signals to others that superiors are not confident in the female manager's capabilities. Consequently, this undercuts her authority and no one takes her seriously. It practically invites others to look for signs of failure and to undercut her.

Even when female managers are respected for their competence and expertise, others may still assume they should bypass them when making important decisions because these women are *not connected* with those on the inside and don't really know the ropes. An unusual dilemma has been created here. Even though women may be respected for their competence or expertise, they are not necessarily seen as being informed beyond the technical requirements of the job. This reaction is partly in response to the staff and other "outsider" types of jobs usually held by women before becoming part of management. Another reason is that business clubs and even company business lunches have typically excluded women. Consequently, women usually seek out each other for support or informal socializing. Regardless of the reasons, however, any woman seen as organizationally naive and lacking organizational support will not be taken seriously and will find her avenues of communication limited.

Even when women are able to achieve some power, they have not always been able to translate this personal credibility into a strong organizational power base. To create a network of supporters, it is required that a manager pass on and share power, and that her subordinates and peers be empowered by virtue of their connection with her. Effective interpersonal power often comes from emphasizing the dignity of others and keeping one's own sense of importance from becoming inflated.

To build a *political support base*, female managers need to share the credit and act as collegial facilitators. Traditionally, however, neither men nor women have seen women as capable of sponsoring others; rather, women have been viewed as the recipients of sponsorship. Thus, a female manager's female subordinates may actually see her as a hindrance to their own careers rather than as a team facilitator.

For example, take the dilemma presented by Laura, a woman who at age 31 is head of corporate communications for a growing computer company:

> I have a huge budget, full authority over my staff, a good salary, plus excellent fringe benefits and the confidence of management. I have little trouble being taken seriously by male superiors or subordinates. But, for some reason, women are my worst enemies. I play by the rules, try to be fair, helpful, and supportive. Yet, it seems as if every decision I make is challenged behind my back. What am I doing wrong? Or am I simply a victim of jealousy?

Laura feels she plays by the rules and doesn't know why her female subordinates are undermining her authority. Chances are she is doing nothing unusual as a department manager, especially since male subordinates respond well to her leadership. Laura's problem reflects some women's inexperience in dealing with each other in a nonsocial, nonsexual environment.

Laura's age may be a factor in her dilemma; but it is probably not her youth as much as her attitude that makes her a target. Not all of the women born in the 1950s escaped the traditional female sex-role conditioning. Laura's age group of young female managers who feel they are entitled to hold responsible jobs and are not guilt-ridden about career advancements can be a threat to the women who are "victims" of more traditional sex-role conditioning.

Many of the political difficulties of female managers are a result of the inexperience that surrounds them. Some women may not grasp the significance of the hierarchical system. If, for example, a female manager finds that the secretaries don't ever "get to" her work and/or her authority is undermined by public criticism, it may be that contempt is being expressed for her and/or her rank. It may also be that a personality conflict, sexism, ageism, jealousy, or a variety of other human emotions are operating. It is important to be aware of these factors because they can get in the way of her political clout and career advancement.

SOURCES OF POWER FOR WOMEN MANAGERS

Samuel Johnson once said that "nature has given women so much power that the law has very wisely given them little." Historically, this is true. Women have exerted their power mainly through informal relationships, while men have dominated formal power positions in armies, governments, and business organizations.[4] These differences in formal power are usually explained as differences in childhood socialization where boys were rewarded for competitive aggressive behavior and girls were expected to be passive and accommodating. If female managers want to achieve equal power in organizations without waiting for a new generation of female managers to arise who have not been subjected to as much traditional sex-role socialization, then they are going to have to take an active stance now in changing the existing organizational climate. One of the variables which can be utilized in this pursuit is the active manipulation of the basic power sources themselves.

Power is the means to get things done. According to Deaux, power depends on both the perceived and real influence both inside and outside the work group.[5] **Influence** is any psychological force which can cause a change in another person. In the case of a manager, influence is initiated by an interpersonal transaction consisting of some form of communication, whether verbal, written, or behavioral. **Interpersonal power** is the ability to get another person to do something spontaneously that he or she would not have done necessarily.[6]

The greater the number of influence sources available to a female manager, the greater her potential power. French and Raven have described the six commonly accepted bases of social power discussed below. These are: (1) legitimate power, (2) reward power, (3) coercive power, (4) referent power, (5) expert power, and (6) information power.[7]

Legitimate Power

Based on authority vested in a position or role in an organization, **legitimate power** belongs to the person who holds that position. This is a legally or socially acceptable form of power which is a part of the unwritten contract agreed upon when individuals join an organization. It is also backed by a system of rewards and punishments which the manager may apply according to legitimate role expectations.

Since men, historically and currently, tend to hold the highest positions in organizations, they also have a greater degree of legitimate power than women. However, as more women rise to formal positions of authority in organizations, they will increase their share of legitimate power. Thus, legitimate power should lose its predominantly masculine connotation.

Both male and female managers at the same level in an organizational hierarchy have the same degree of legitimate power because their positions and associated degrees of authority are equivalent. However, their actual ability to influence, motivate, and direct the work of subordinates may differ widely according to their personal sources of power.

Reward Power

Reward power is the ability to compensate and give rewards to individuals who satisfactorily complete assigned tasks. It is based on the expectation that, if a subordinate conforms to a directive, he or she will receive a reward which may be in a formal form like money, public praise, or a promotion; or in an informal form like acceptance, self-confirmation, or attention.

Formal rewards are usually perceived as masculine modes of influence and are thought to be more effective when employed by male managers.[8] In order for women to use formal rewards as an effective power base, they must first have access to high positions of authority in the organization. In the meantime, however, informal rewards can be very effective in building a reciprocal social network.

Coercive Power

The ability to punish is called **coercive power**. The influence of coercive power is based on fear and the perception that subordinates will be punished if they do not conform to the manager's directives. Coercive power may take the form of physical or verbal abuse, withdrawal of desired treatment or sentiments, or withdrawal of valued resources.

Coercive power, although the opposite of reward power, is also usually perceived as a masculine mode of influence.[9] The generally lower status of women in the organizational hierarchy is the main impediment to their effective use of formal punishment as a power base. However, punishment can be effectively utilized by women in many informal ways, such as withdrawing emotional support, avoidance, or lack of personal interest.

Referent Power

Referent power is based upon the attractiveness and appeal of individuals that causes them to be liked personally. Others imitate the personal style or behavior of someone with referent power because of their respect or liking for that person. It results in friendship, positive sentiments, reciprocal affection, and positive expectations. A leader who is admired and followed because of referent power is said to have charisma. Examples of charismatic individuals are John F. Kennedy, Jane Fonda, and Golda Meir.

Referent power is particularly effective for women in nontraditional occupations because it has not been sex-role stereotyped as either a masculine or feminine power base.[10] People with referent power are respected for their competence and personal characteristics regardless of their formal authority in the organization.

Expert Power

The influence accorded to a manager who has superior knowledge, ability, or skill is known as **expert power**. These bases of expertise may be obtained through special training, experience, access to rare information, exceptional abilities, or just a general aura of competence.

Expert power stems from the abilities of the individual and it is not necessarily related to formal position in the organization. Because expertise emphasizes competence and can be easily generalized, it is especially valuable to women managers endeavoring to enhance their organizational power base.

Information Power

The influence people have when they possess information that is valuable to others who don't have it is referred to as **information power**. Although expertise can be based on special information, anyone who possesses information of any type desired by others has information power.

Like expertise, information is not necessarily based on formal position in an organization. Information power comes from formal or informal information which may be held by high- or low-level organization members.

Information power can be coercive power when facts are withheld that are necessary to another's effectiveness or satisfaction. It can be rewarding when information vital to important decisions is shared freely. Managers who share their information in positive ways are usually well-liked and thought to be highly competent by subordinates.[11]

A new manager automatically inherits legitimate power because of the authority associated with that position. Although authority is a legitimate possession, exercising the right to command others is a complex process in which the best interests of both the organization and the individuals involved must be considered if it is to be an effective base of power. Authority in a managerial position is often limited to the job description, the management-union contract, and the degree of acceptance by subordinates. **Earned authority**, on the other hand, refers to the totality of power which is derived through one's competence, valued contributions, and individual character. It is much more persuasive than that conferred by the legitimate authority alone. In the long run, a woman manager, like male managers, needs power gained through acceptance and support in order to accomplish desired results.

Since legitimate power is limited to the authority inherent in a position, the effective woman manager must take maximum advantage of reward, coercive, referent, expert, and information power potentials. Personal influence is more important and broader than formal authority, for it is based on one's capability to personally persuade people to act in such a way that they promote the accomplishment of the organization's goals. The key to being effective in influencing others is not so much the formal authority of the manager's position but the authority she earns through the effective use of the other types of power discussed above. Other skills described in this book are of key importance to enhancing her earned authority with subordinates. Some examples are the image she projects (Chapter 3) and the communication skills that she utilizes (Chapter 6).

POWER AND THE WOMAN MANAGER'S CAREER

A recent *Business Week* magazine survey of 43 corporations found that, in spite of over a decade of affirmative action, steady pressure by women's groups, and increasing acceptance by corporate men, the top-rung women executives in most organizations are in middle management. Even though women with MBA degrees receive higher starting salaries on the average than their male counterparts, they are soon surpassed by men in both salary and rank as experience is accumulated.[12]

Because of many of the "power failures" described previously, most women managers find themselves in "velvet ghettos"—stuck in areas where women have typically been regarded as best suited. For example, women are clustered in staff functions like personnel, corporate social responsibility, or public relations which are peripheral to the more directly powerful line functions like sales, production, or finance. Thus, many women come to rest full circle in the same type of positions which inhibited their building of an adequate power base in the first place. Nevertheless, having these positions does allow for the satisfaction of many women's career aspirations and avoids affirmative-action pressures on the company. At the same time, these positions preserve the existing balance of power that favors the males in the organization.

Although an abundance of opportunities exists in the stereotypically female management areas like consumer relations or public relations, specializing in these areas because they represent the easiest path for advancement is not always the best career-development strategy for women. Three alternative career strategies, their advantages, disadvantages, and respective power bases are presented in Figure 7-1.

Using Feminine Characteristics to Advantage

The manager's strategy of using feminine characteristics to her advantage in positions and career paths places high value on such qualities as social sensitivity, helpfulness, humanitarian values, and awareness of feelings. These qualities may be viewed as

FIGURE 7-1

POWER BASES AND CAREER-DEVELOPMENT STRATEGIES AVAILABLE TO WOMEN MANAGERS

Strategy	Power Bases Emphasized	Advantages	Disadvantages
Use perceptions of feminine characteristics to advantage	Expert and informational	Easily assimilated into prevailing masculine culture Takes advantage of opportunities presently available in socially oriented functions May be benefactor of increased importance attached to socially oriented functions	Supports stereotyping of women as unfit for management Leads to obtaining staff positions typically peripheral to more powerful line positions May lead to dead-end jobs and career stagnation after initial successes
Adopt masculine standard of behavior	Referent	Easily assimilated into prevailing masculine culture Precedent established for using this strategy May succeed if adhered to rigidly	Supports stereotyping of women as unfit for management Initially gives up referent power Lends to conflict between sexual identity and career identity for some women

FIGURE 7-1 (Continued)

Strategy	Power Bases Emphasized	Advantages	Disadvantages
Seek entry into "old boys' network"	Referent, coercive, and reward	More active strategy and reflects less passivity Complementary to other strategies and may be simultaneously pursued If successful, power is held in both formal and informal systems	May find resistance to women in "old boys' network" Results not immediately forthcoming Maintenance of membership and particular relationship requires energy beyond that devoted to the job If unsuccessful, may hinder career more than if entry was not attempted

relative strengths by both male and female superiors who are influential in her career advancement. If she decides to concentrate on this strategy, cultivating the "feminine qualities" expected and developing the associated specialized knowledge may provide her with considerable influence in important corporate decisions.

Adopting a Masculine Style of Behavior

By conforming to the masculine stereotype, women fit the dominant profile of the traditional successful manager. This strategy seems to be easiest for young females just starting their managerial careers. A study of female MBAs, all of whom were under 30 years of age and held jobs in business, found that these female managers described themselves in more masculine than feminine terms, as did their male counterparts. However, this masculine self-image may not be as easy to assimilate for older women who have seen themselves all of their lives in much more feminine ways.[14]

Seeking Entry into "Old Boys' Network"

This action-oriented strategy of seeking entry into the "old boys' network" enhances the woman manager's power base by *breaking into areas of influence dominated by men*. Studies have shown that women typically tend to focus on self-improvement as the critical strategy in career advancement. Unfortunately this is a *passive*, "wait to be chosen" approach which ignores the political realities of such decisions and assumes a powerless position from which to initiate changes themselves.[14]

An associated strategy for building support is to set up an informal women's group or large-scale female network. Although these groupings provide a feeling of belongingness and opportunities for exchanging ideas, they still keep women out of the "old boys' network" where the real sources of power are reserved.

Entering into existing male networks is a much more active strategy which requires a lot more assertiveness and ability to handle resistance. If the woman manager is successful, however, the rewards are tremendous. She will make connections with the most influential people. She will understand and be part of the key political systems, and will be able to use her connections and knowledge to wield acknowledged power with anyone in the organization.

None of the three strategies mentioned above will work equally well for all women. Each assumes implicitly that women are operating from an initial power base of competence and that they are seeking to build on it. The feasibility and ultimate success of any strategy depends upon the prevailing culture of the organization and the additional power bases a woman manager can bring into play.

STRATEGIES FOR ENHANCING INTERPERSONAL POWER

The majority of women managers do not yet occupy positions of formal authority allowing them an adequate legitimate power base in organizations. Consequently, those women who are more influential tend to build their power bases from the more personal sources of expertise, information, and charisma. Some of the more subtle strategies for building the woman manager's interpersonal power base are summarized below.[15]

Be Assertive

Don't hesitate to seize power when opportunities arise. Someone must be in charge before anything can even get started. Therefore, although the manager may find office politics and the responsibility of power distasteful, she may wind up being manipulated by others who are more aggressive if she doesn't seize the opportunity.

Submissive speech patterns give power away.[16] Take the nonassertive woman asking for a raise. "I hate to ask, but would it be all right if I asked for a raise," she asks her boss in a weak voice with her eyes on the floor. Although her boss has a perfect right to say no, she should ask for that raise like she deserves it and has a right to it. If she asks for something assertively, her boss—and others—will take her more seriously, and she's got a much better chance of getting what she wants.

Be Courteous

Being courteous and cordial to people, even if one doesn't like them, is as important as being good at the job one does. Managers usually come to expect at least nominal deference from those in lower positions. This doesn't mean that employees have to sell out their values or throw away their pride to keep a manager happy, or that the manager has to do the same to keep her superiors happy.

But energy should be expended to maintain everyone's integrity and pride. This can be accomplished if discussions are carried on constructively and differences worked through until people agree, as opposed to being forced into submissive positions via inappropriate use of formal power.

Courtesy is one of the most effective tools for getting things done. Courtesy in this context is the act of making others feel good or powerful in one's relationship with them. Since the majority of a manager's subordinates will probably fall toward the passive end of the power scale, it is important to reinforce their self-esteem frequently to keep them at their most productive level.

Courtesy is also important for the manager's own career development since discourteous people seldom progress up the organizational ladder. It helps to keep the manager's superior happy. Although this may sound self-serving, it is vital for the manager's own success to have a happy, self-assured superior who is confident of her competence and support. She can't afford either a wishy-washy agreement or an arbitrary nay-saying! But if she acts in a courteous, cordial manner, she will be more respected and have a better chance of having her opinions count.

Direct Your Thinking

One should plan, organize, and direct one's own thinking. Directed thinking means clearly specifying what it is one hopes to accomplish in an interpersonal situation and systematically considering all factors which may help in achieving it. Spontaneity is often good for building strong, interpersonal relationships; but it can also hurt people if one is not careful. For example, when one insults others without thinking, it often is very difficult or impossible to undo the damage. In this case it is too late for hindsight unless one transfers the lessons learned to another situation. It is better to use directed thinking to gain the foresight to prevent any undue damage in the first place.

The following questions can help the manager select and organize meaningful information so that she can behave in a directed way:

1. How has this person or group reacted to similar situations?

2. Which approaches worked in the past? Which ones did not?

3. How does this person or group feel about me? How can I influence this impression?

4. How does this person or group feel about the change being proposed? What is the person's or group's point of view? Why?

5. What is the most effective way of communicating?

6. What unique considerations are relevant to this person or group in this situation?

Neutralize Resistance

One should use disclaimers to neutralize resistance to one's ideas. The context in which the manager is interacting has a great deal of influence on others' reactions. If other people involved feel that she will personally benefit from her own request for a specific course of action, they may feel that they are being ripped off for her personal gain. To counter this attitude, she needs to "disclaim" their feeling that she is requesting something just for her personal benefit. If she will benefit from the action, she needs to own up to this but convince others that it is also a good thing for them regardless of her situation. By owning up to her situation—which they are aware of anyway—others may be disarmed by her sincerity and realize that she is leveling with them and not trying to pull the wool over their eyes. Then they can listen to what she has to say without constantly being on guard to detect what they expect to be her own hidden agenda. It sometimes helps in these circumstances to present a more balanced account of the situation and the strategies she is suggesting to demonstrate that she has done a thorough investigation regardless of her emotional concerns.

Inoculate the Key Decision Makers

If one is fairly certain that other influential key decision makers will later attempt to refute one's requests, it is a good idea to try and inoculate them against arguments so as to change their minds. This strategy often can be used by sharing possible counterarguments with decision makers and demonstrating the fallacies of these counterarguments. This technique tends to build resistance to further opposition to one's requests.

Use the Media

Media dissemination of one's ideas and proposals to others in the organization through memos or bulletin announcements is a relatively risk-free strategy which may be effective in gaining the support of influential organization members. It is a good approach to use to raise awareness about a problem and to start people thinking of ideas to solve it. The same thing can be done on a smaller scale through word of mouth.

Build Support Groups

Support groups consist of organization members who share a common concern for changing some aspect of the organization. They are important for testing ideas, expressing empathy, and supporting one another under heavy opposition. Such group meetings can produce increased awareness about the nature and consequences of a proposed change and provide the manager with a better perspective of how to gain more control within her organization.

Gatekeep

Gatekeeping is a way of controlling the communication process so that everyone concerned has an equal chance to participate and to be heard. Through such simple comments as "What do the rest of you think?" or "We haven't heard from Jim yet," it may be possible for a manager to decrease the influence of some of her more assertive opponents and solicit important information from those who support her and her proposal.

Hold Out

Holding out is a blocking strategy which prevents a decision or calls attention to a negative program that needs one's approval or participation to be successful. Failing to cooperate or to go along with a decision or plan of action is dangerous and unpleasant, but in some situations the risk is necessary for a manager to get her point across.

Go Around

The manager may find herself in a situation where her superior in the organization simply will not agree to consider a change which she feels is vital. Under such conditions, she may feel that her only alternative is to go over her superior's head to gain support. This is a *dangerous* maneuver because it violates the trust of her superior and makes her vulnerable to any sanctions he or she may apply. *Consequently, it should be used very rarely and only in desperate situations.*

Threaten to Resign

The threat of resignation is the manager's ultimate weapon. If she is a valuable manager, her opposition will listen to her when she lays her job on the line. Obviously this is an extremely dangerous strategy, and the warnings administered with respect to going around superiors should be doubled or tripled in this case. She should never cry "wolf" with this strategy. She shouldn't use it unless she means it. If her opposition senses a bluff and calls it, she will forever lose face or her job.

SEX AS A POWER TACTIC

Although we certainly don't condone it, using sex to get power is as old as Cleopatra. Since this tactic is used, an awareness and understanding of it and the full range of its possible consequences are necessary. Using sex as a stepping-stone to power can be as brief as flirting at the drinking fountain or as long-lasting as marrying the boss's son (or daughter). What follows is a description of the four main sexual strategies and examples of such strategies in Horn and Horn's *Sex in the Office*.[17]

Flirtation

Flirting is usually directed toward some powerful person, maybe even the boss himself. If the boss responds in an approving way, the flirt feels singled out and special. If that's all there is to it, nobody cares that much and nobody gets hurt.

A lot of times, however, the original overtones which may have been mildly encouraged become more outrageous, producing one or two unfortunate results. The boss may become embarrassed or tired of the game. Consequently, he slaps the flirt down hard. On the other hand, the boss may take the come-ons too seriously. Either way the flirter's ego and job prospects are both bound to be hurt.

One flirt denied that what she does hurts herself or anyone else. Her rules are to flatter men, help everyone, learn a lot, and move on. Her flirting involves more than sexual titillation—the button strategically left open, the cute smile, the joking innuendo. It includes an offer to always be available to help other powerful people when needed and an investment of time in learning about superiors' hobbies so that she can share their interests. This flirt feels that if she limited herself to her duties, she would be just another young trainee. She believes that moving beyond that requires more than friendliness and hard work. Thus, she believes that a bit of flirting helps.

The office party or picnic is a prime chance for judicious flirting. Flirts know that executives use social occasions to size up the staff informally and that some discretionary flirting may help them get talked to, not talked about, later on.

Dating

Flirting often leads to dating, which is a nonexclusive arrangement that may or may not include sexual intimacy. Power-inspired dating is done with the boss or someone else higher up in the organization. It can open doors to the inner circle and provide the dater with useful information and connections for getting ahead in the job or moving on to a better one.

An attractive assistant to the personnel manager of a large Midwestern conglomerate used dating to help her get the career advancement she wanted. She had learned of a proposed purchase in California which would expand the Midwestern office. In searching for ways to be promoted to the California office, she began dating one of the financial vice-presidents. She deliberately became more involved with the vice-president, who started bringing her to company parties. There she met a variety of top-management people that she hoped would remember her favorably when the time came. She never mentioned her interest in the West Coast until the company formally announced the expansion. Then she wrote to the corporate officials she had met, expressing her interest in being relocated. Her strategy paid off, and within a year she was named personnel manager of the new West Coast division.

This dater does not feel that she did anything wrong to advance her career. Her rationale was that she simply used the best route open to her to get the chance to prove herself. If she had been a man, she said, she might have played golf or kept her ears open in the men's room. But, being an attractive woman, she used that asset instead.

Regardless of the ethics involved, dating the boss or a superior can backfire, especially if higher-ups disapprove of such activities, officially or otherwise. The woman manager will never know when the date may thank her for her attention and favors but think less of her as a competent administrator. *Not* dating superiors is less likely to backfire, even if the organization's culture tolerates these activities. People admire others who live up to their convictions and, generally speaking, these convictions still hold out for "keeping one's love life out of the office." If the woman manager is criticized for not granting a superior's request for a date, she should remember that there are Equal Employment Opportunities Commission guidelines on sexual harassment.

Flings

Short-term, hotly paced sexual interludes are another ploy in the quest for power. A young graduate student once admitted to becoming involved with every member of her dissertation committee in order to insure a favorable response to her doctoral dissertation. Others have reported that a single fling is adequate if it's with the right person, at the right time, and accomplished in a sophisticated atmosphere. Their rationale is that the memory of a pleasant fling will help the boss see them in a favorable light when it's time for a promotion or a raise. On the other hand, the boss may feel that a bed partner already received her bonus for the year!

Affairs

Affairs are the next step up the power scale after dating and flings. They are exclusive, longer-term sexual relationships. They are the ultimate sex-to-gain-power ploy because they are more intense and continuous than other strategies, and because they provide more opportunities for getting and using power.

At the beginning, both partners usually are getting something that they need. Usually she wants to be noticed and to enter part of the world which she feels is otherwise closed to her. He usually wants to be admired and looked up to by a pretty woman. Using an affair to get what they want does work for some of the people some of the time. Since people who deliberately use sex for power are not usually looking for true love, any outcome that increases their power stands to be successful.

As with any sexual strategy, affairs are wrought with danger. They are fairly easy to begin but more difficult to continue, and usually very difficult to break off without someone getting hurt either on the job, off the job, or both. Furthermore, it is usually the woman who pays, although that is changing nowadays.

Take the following case where everyone paid. An account executive and his assistant were having an affair, during which he promised her a promotion. As time passed, passions cooled and the promised promotion was forgotten. The assistant quit, but not before she copied documents from her boss's files revealing questionable actions against a competitor. She passed on the copies and her revenge resulted in a lose-lose outcome for all involved, and even some who weren't.

The readers of this book have probably heard stories of women who have slept their way to the top, using sex as a stepping-stone up the corporate ladder. In actuality, these stories are usually just that—stories based on a desire to denigrate the accomplishments of someone else—or wishful thinking. But even stories can have devasting effects, as in the case mentioned earlier about Mary Cunningham and Bill Agee, chairman of the board at Bendix Corporation. Her rapid rise from an MBA recruit to a top administrative position in less than a year, and her frequent appearances with the boss, started rumors about how Cunningham accomplished so much so fast and eventually cost her her job.[18]

When a power-motivated affair works as planned, the reward can be a promotion, a raise, or easier working conditions. Rewards also include the power associated with being on the inside and backed up by the boss. However, very often one or both partners, and sometimes innocent bystanders, end up getting hurt. Although affairs do take place, the aggrandizement of this exciting play for power should be carefully weighed against the possible long-term consequences.

ACTION GUIDELINES

Both acquiring and properly applying power are important issues for women managers who, for the most part, come from backgrounds which ignore or downplay power for women, or that promote more passive postures. Power and politics are realities of organizational life, and successfully coping with them is vital to managerial and career success. The following guidelines are helpful for the manager in acquiring and using power effectively.

1. Avoid peripheral job assignments and seek out those allowing maximum exposure and realistic challenge.
2. Avoid overprotective superiors and those who are cynical toward women's capabilities in general. If avoidance is not possible, the manager should try to clarify her expectations as soon as possible.
3. Use feminine characteristics to advantage, adopt masculine behaviors where appropriate, and make inroads in male-dominated networks.
4. For maximum gain, build power from legitimate, reward, coercive, referent, expert, and informational sources simultaneously.
5. Be aware of how sex is used in power politics, but be wary of using it personally.

FOOTNOTES

1. P. D. Horn and J. C. Horn, *Sex in the Office* (Reading, MA: Addison-Wesley, 1982).

2. *Ibid.*

3. R. M. Kanter, "Power Failure in Management Circuits," *Harvard Business Review* (July-August, 1979), pp. 65-75.

4. N. Colwill, *The New Partnership: Women and Men in Organizations* (Palo Alto, CA: Mayfield Publishing Co., 1982).

5. K. Deaux, "Authority, Gender, Power, and Tokenism," *The Journal of Applied Behavioral Sciences*, 14 (January-March, 1978), pp. 22-25.

6. P. Johnson, "Women and Power: Toward A Theory of Effectiveness," *The Journal of Social Issues*, Vol. 32, 3 (1976), pp. 99-110.

7. J. R. P. French and B. Raven, "The Bases of Social Power," in D. Cartwright (ed.), *Studies in Social Power* (Ann Arbor, MI: University of Michigan, 1959), pp. 150-167.

8. B. Rosen and T. H. Jerdee, "The Influence of Sex-Role Stereotypes on Evaluations of Male and Female Supervisory Behavior," *Journal of Applied Psychology*, Vol. 57 (1973), pp. 44-48.

9. L. A. Dunn, "Consideration of Variables in Reward and Coercive Influence Attempts" (Unpublished manuscript, Tufts University, Medford, MA. 1972).

10. P. Johnson, "Social Power and Sex Role Stereotyping" (Doctoral dissertation, University of California, Los Angeles, 1974).

11. T. Litman-Adizes, G. Fontaine, and B. H. Raven, "Consequences of Social Power and Causal Attribution for Compliance As Seen by Powerholder and Target," *Personality and Social Psychology Bulletin*, Vol. 4, No. 2 (1978), pp. 260-264.

12. G. N. Powell, "Career Development and the Woman Manager—A Social Power Perspective," *Personnel* (May-June, 1980), pp. 22-32.

13. *Ibid.*

14. *Ibid.*

15. Adapted from L. Sperry, D. J. Nicholson, and P. L. Hunsaker, *You Can Make It Happen: A Guide to Self-Actualization and Organizational Change* (Reading, MA: Addison-Wesley, 1977), pp. 186-192.

16. Liz Houston, "Businesswomanly Wile: A Few Rules on Disarming the Skeptic," *MBA* (September, 1977).

17. Horn and Horn, *op. cit.*

18. M. Cunningham, *Powerplay: What Really Happened at Bendix* (New York: Simon and Schuster, 1984).

CHAPTER 8

Working Effectively with Groups

OUTLINE

I.   Delegating
   A.   Reasons for Ineffective Delegating
   B.   Useful Principles of Delegating

II. Problems of Women in Groups
   A.   Sex Ratios of Groups
   B.   Overcoming of Female Stereotypes in Male-Dominated Groups
      1.   The "Mass and Model" Approach
      2.   Effective Management of Groups

III. Key Group Processes
   A.   Communication Patterns
   B.   Decision-Making Procedures
   C.   Group Role Behaviors
      1.   Task Role Behaviors
      2.   Maintenance Role Behaviors
      3.   Self-Oriented Role Behaviors
   D.   Emotional Issues
      1.   Identity
      2.   Control and Power
      3.   Goals
      4.   Acceptance and Intimacy

IV. Emotional Behaviors and Styles
   A.   Types of Emotional Behavior
      1.   A Show of Tough Emotions
      2.   A Show of Tender Emotions
      3.   A Denial of All Emotion
   B.   Types of Emotional Styles
      1.   The Friendly Helper Style
      2.   The Tough Battler Style
      3.   The Logical Thinker Style

V.   Group Strengths and Weaknesses
   A.   Advantages of Groups in Decision Making
   B.   Weaknesses of Groups in Decision Making
   C.   Guidelines for Achieving a Group's Potential

VI. Conducting Effective Meetings

Action Guidelines

In the previous chapter we discussed the importance of power for managers as they relate to their superiors. In this chapter we begin with the importance of *delegating* as a means of building power by giving away some power to subordinates. Then we deal with ways in which managers can work effectively with groups of peers and subordinates.

DELEGATING

One way of building a network of political supporters is for the manager to pass on and share her power with others who are qualified. This builds trust and support between her and her subordinates which can be translated into increased referent power. Unfortunately most female managers resist delegation, and this hampers their effectiveness in business. When similar difficulties have been studied among male managers, it has been demonstrated that the inability to delegate ranks very high in contributing to the mortality of managerial careers.[1]

Most successful male executives don't hesitate to break large projects down into a lot of small, manageable parts and parcel out these pieces to others. They carefully hand out details they do not want to handle personally, as well as other tasks considered to be potentially dangerous to their own careers. They also quickly delegate work that is tedious, time-consuming, or unlikely to be noticed by top management.

Women, on the other hand, generally hang on to every bit of an assignment, even though it may be overwhelming. They check and recheck every detail, making sure that everything is done perfectly. This means that their own hands stay too full to take on bigger and better things.

Reasons for Ineffective Delegating

Many a manager has probably uttered one or more of the following statements:[2]

♦   It's easier to do it myself, and I know it will be done right if I do it.

- I don't have enough confidence in my subordinates.
- I'm afraid of what my boss will think.
- I like to get personal credit for these tasks.
- I thought I had plenty of time to do it myself.
- I'm afraid the worker will think I'm imposing on him or her.

Ineffective delegating can occur for a variety of reasons. Sometimes the manager is eager to prove her ability and demonstrate her assertiveness in doing things her way. At other times, she just may be impatient with subordinates for taking too long to accomplish results for which she feels responsible.

Although it is understandable that managers want to show early results, not allowing subordinates sufficient time to do a thorough job may be damaging to a climate of trust and teamwork. For delegation to be effective, it helps to explain what has to be done and why, and then allow the subordinates to determine how to do the task and how long it will take them to do a quality job.

An *unwillingness to delegate* is usually the main cause of the problem, as opposed to inability or lack of skill in delegating. Unwillingness is most often based on the desire to hold on to every facet of the job that the manager is responsible for and to avoid potential risks in allowing other people to complete the tasks originally assigned to her. There may be even greater risks, however, if she does not delegate appropriately. By delegating to others, she can multiply herself and take on other more important activities. Delegating effectively involves priorities, setting realistic deadlines, and managing her own time effectively.

For the subordinates, delegating has both personal and job-related values. Delegating can help them increase their confidence, assess their capabilities, and enhance their understanding of the business as a whole. Delegating appropriate decisions to subordinates may also lead to better decisions since they are often closest to the firing line and have a better view of what is needed. It has also been shown that accepting responsibility and having opportunities to exercise judgment make subordinates' jobs more satisfying and increase their commitment to accomplishing organizational goals.

Useful Principles of Delegating

If the manager has developed an effective work team, she will be able to dismiss the feeling of insecurity that tasks which she delegates may not be done right. Also, she will not have to fear the loss of power if subordinates do a good job. Mutual confidence between managers and subordinates is an important foundation for effective delegation to take place. Within an atmosphere of mutual support, the following useful principles of delegation have been established:[3]

1. *Establish goals.* The manager should clarify the objectives and the importance of the tasks being delegated. This includes the amount of effort that will be involved, the expected completion date, and the desired end product.

2. *Define responsibility and authority.* The manager should build the necessary legitimate power and information power into the delegated assignment and make it known to the subordinate and others involved that this authority has been delegated. Subordinates should also be clearly informed about what they will be held accountable for.

3. *Establish adequate controls.* The manager should make sure that subordinates know her standards and expectations. She should provide the yardsticks by which she can judge the caliber of completed work. In order to avoid spending all of her time checking on how subordinates are doing, she should provide a reliable control system such as weekly reports or informal interim meetings for periodic discussion and evaluation.

4. *Provide training.* First, the manager should be sure the subordinate to whom she has assigned a task is willing to take it on and is able to handle it. She should be certain that the subordinate has the necessary experience, education, and judgment to do the job. The subordinate may also require some additional training to enhance job performance. These steps will reduce the element of risk involved by assuring assignments to subordinates with adequate skills and attitudes.

5. *Motivate subordinates.* The extra responsibility of delegated tasks is not always enough to encourage all subordinates to accept and perform well. The manager should be sensitive to the specific needs and goals of subordinates and provide individual incentives for doing the delegated task well.

6. *Require completed work.* When a task is delegated to a subordinate, he or she has the responsibility to complete the task appropriately. The manager's job is to provide guidance, help, and necessary information. It does her little good if she receives back from subordinates incomplete work which she must essentially redo herself.

PROBLEMS OF WOMEN IN GROUPS

"When a man is the rarity in a group, he is likely to be central, to be deferred to and respected. When a woman is the rarity, she is likely to be isolated, to be treated as trivial."[4] Effective intervention in such situations depends upon understanding these dynamics as a function of the group and not necessarily of the individuals involved. Consequently, for a female manager who must still spend a great deal of time interacting in meetings as a minority, it is of key importance to be aware of the ramifications of sex differences in groups and to possess the knowledge and skills necessary to be an effective member under these circumstances.

Because of traditional stereotypes and the relatively recent addition of women to male-dominated groups, females face special problems regardless of their skills as group members. The effective implementation and demonstration of these skills, however, can go a long way in overcoming biased expectations and in facilitating acceptance as a competent group member.

Sex Ratios of Groups

Recent research has confirmed the commonsense knowledge that all-male, all-female, and mixed-sex groups differ in their content, process, and relationship styles.[5] All-male groups tend to exhibit more competition, practical joking, avoidance of intimacy, and impersonality than all-female groups. All-female groups, on the other hand, demonstrate more affiliation, concern about relationships, personal references, and concern about family than all-male groups.

In mixed-sex groups, men become more tense, serious, self-conscious, less competitive, and reduce practical joking. Both men and women become more personal and share more feelings, but women speak less often than men. Sexual tensions usually develop, and concerns are felt about being attractive to the opposite sex.

If the ratio of men to women is relatively equal in a group, both sexes will experience the emotional issues of identity, power, goals, and acceptance (discussed later in this chapter) with increased intensity because of the factors just described. If a woman is the only female in a male-dominated group, however, her performance may be hindered because of additional typecastings.

Overcoming of Female Stereotypes in Male-Dominated Groups

The stereotyped female roles (mother, seductress, pet, and iron maiden) discussed in Chapter 1 are, of course, caricatures. However, their more subtle, real-life applications all serve to isolate the solitary woman from the mainstream of group interaction and prevent her from demonstrating her competencies. It is extremely difficult for a solitary woman to break out of these roles because the absence of other women from the group often leads her to believe that her future lies in being successful, along with the men, according to their expectations.

The "Mass and Model" Approach. Rosabeth Kanter has proposed the "mass and model" approach which gives women several possible solutions to overcoming these stereotypes and exercising their full competence freely.[6] First, the female manager can *talk openly* in the group about these sex-role and majority-minority problems. Second, she should seek out *female role models* in powerful positions in her own organization or in others. Those female role models may be able to provide her with specific feedback and advice. Using them as examples in her group can change her own image through association. Finally, whenever possible, she should include a "critical mass" of females in every work group. If *more than two or three women* can be included in large work groups, they can help reduce stereotyping without threatening one another. It's true that there is strength in numbers and, as enough people expose outdated stereotypes and unproductive group expectations, it is possible to positively change the culture of the group for all participants.

Effective Management of Groups. Most people have participated in work groups with a variety of problems, in addition to specific female issues. This experience has led many managers to the conclusion that groups are inevitably inefficient, time-consuming, and ineffective. At other times, however, many people have participated in highly effective and creative work groups, which demonstrates that groups have many advantages if they are managed effectively. The advantages and disadvantages of groups in decision making are discussed later in this chapter.

To be effective when working with groups, at least two things are necessary. First, the manager needs to be aware of the fundamentals of group dynamics so that she can *understand* the meaning of what is going on. In a meeting, for example, many things in addition to the words being spoken influence the group's effectiveness. Examples are roles, hidden agendas, emotions, and nonverbal behavior. Second, she needs to be able to apply this understanding to avoid problems and capitalize on strengths in order to make group situations more effective.

KEY GROUP PROCESSES

This section provides a synopsis of the key group processes described by Kolb, Rubin, and McIntyre in the areas of (1) communication patterns, (2) decision-making procedures, (3) group role behaviors, and (4) emotional issues.[7] The remainder of this chapter will present ideas on how to capitalize on the strengths of groups and avoid the weaknesses of groups in making decisions. The ability to learn how to apply this knowledge to conduct more effective meetings will also be discussed.

Communication Patterns

One of the easiest aspects of group processes to observe is the pattern of communication. The kind of observations people make gives them clues to other important things that may be going on in the group such as who leads whom, who influences whom, who likes or dislikes whom, and how positive and optimistic the group members feel about the task and about one another. The communication variables to be aware of include the following:

1. Who talks?

2. For how long?

3. How often? (Time is a limited resource and those who tend to use more of it oftentimes are more influential.)

4. Whom do people look at when they talk? (The possibilities are: (a) *individuals*, especially potential supporters or people whose evaluation is critical; (b) the *group*, in order to read reactions of the entire audience; and (c) *nobody*, often when trying to disguise hidden motives.)

5. Who talks after whom, and who interrupts whom? (More powerful and/or more caring people react differently from others.)

6. What style of communication is used by way of assertions, questions, tone of voice, etc.? (Are people helping and cooperative, or hindering and competing?)

7. Is body language—posture, gestures, seating arrangement—strongly evident? (This is where the emotional messages are.)

These communication patterns will vary according to the sex composition of a group. If there is a lone male in the group, for example, he will probably tend to talk more and receive most of the attention. A lone female, on the other hand, is often ignored or treated as trivial. The style of communication in mixed-sex groups tends to be less aggressive and more accepting than in all-male groups, but female members generally speak much less than males.

Decision-Making Procedures

Whether people are aware of it or not, groups are making decisions all the time. Some of these decisions are made without much awareness, even when they affect vital group procedures or standards of operation. It is important to observe how decisions are made in a group in order to assess the appropriateness of the decision to the matter being decided on. Some methods of decision making and their consequences are listed below.

1. The **plop** is an assertive statement followed by silence. In essence, it is a decision not to do whatever was suggested. For example, "I think we should appoint Fran, the first woman on our committee, as our new chairperson." Silence ensues. The group then moves to another issue, or another person is nominated. The suggested decision has not been accepted. It has plopped.

2. The **self-authorized agenda** is an assertive statement followed by self-initiated action. For example, "I think we should introduce ourselves. My name is Bill Smith . . .," or "I think we need a secretary. Julie, since you're the only woman here, you're it." If Julie acquiesced and the meeting continued along, the decision was made by a self-authorized agenda.

3. When two people support each other to initiate a decision, the **handclasp** occurs. For example, Person A says, "I wonder if it would be helpful if we had someone to take notes." Person B then reaffirms Person A's statement with, "I think it would and, since Fran is the only woman here, let's have her do it." If no one resists this suggestion, and Fran begins to take notes, the handclasp has been effective.

4. The **minority decision** is made when, by asserting their agreement, a "together few" influence an "untogether whole." For example, someone may say, "Does anyone

object?" or "We all agree, don't we?" The silence which usually follows is assumed to imply agreement. In reality, some members of the group may not have had time to decide or check for support from others.

5. The **majority-minority voting** is simply a form of "majority wins" voting. Since women are usually minorities in groups, this means that they usually lose on female-related issues. In any case, the ideas, rationale, and feelings among the group are not processed in a simple show of hands.

6. The **polling method** seeks to find out what everyone thinks about an issue. Depending upon how favorably the outcome is perceived, the initiator may use the results as if a decision had been reached. For example, "Let's see where everyone stands on making Julie the coordinator. What do you think Jim? (pause for Jim's response,) Margaret?" and so on.

7. The **consensus-testing method** consists of a genuine exploration to test for any opposition and to determine whether the opposition feels strongly enough to refuse to implement a decision. It does not necessarily call for unanimity, but an essential agreement by all is achieved.

Since women tend to be the minority in most managerial groups and do not command a proportionate amount of air time regardless of the sex composition of the groups, the female manager's influence in group decisions is jeopardized with all except the *consensus* form of group decision making. As will be pointed out in the next section, judicious use of gatekeeping roles can help women in minority positions make sure that their opinions are heard and counted.

Group Role Behaviors

Behavior in a group (see Figure 8-1) can be classified in terms of what the purpose or function of the behavior seems to be.[8] When a member says something, is that member primarily trying to get the group task accomplished (*task*)? Is the member trying to improve or patch up some relationship among members (*maintenance*)? Or is the member primarily meeting some personal need or goal without regard for the group's problems (*self-oriented*)? Behavior sets aimed at accomplishing some objective in any of these areas are called **roles**.

FIGURE 8-1

TYPES OF GROUP ROLE BEHAVIORS

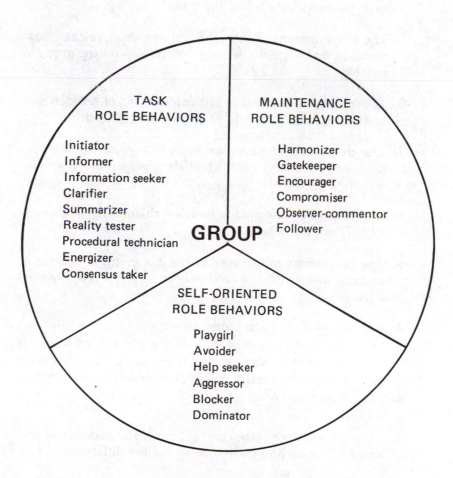

TASK
ROLE BEHAVIORS

Initiator
Informer
Information seeker
Clarifier
Summarizer
Reality tester
Procedural technician
Energizer
Consensus taker

MAINTENANCE
ROLE BEHAVIORS

Harmonizer
Gatekeeper
Encourager
Compromiser
Observer-commentor
Follower

GROUP

SELF-ORIENTED
ROLE BEHAVIORS

Playgirl
Avoider
Help seeker
Aggressor
Blocker
Dominator

Task Role Behaviors. The most common types of role behavior relevant to the group's fulfillment of its *task* are briefly described below.

1. The **initiator** proposes tasks, goals, or actions; defines group problems; and suggests procedures.

2. The **informer** offers facts, gives expression of feelings, and gives opinions.

3. The **information seeker** asks for opinions or facts.

4. The **clarifier** interprets ideas or suggestions, defines terms, and clarifies issues before the group.

5. The **summarizer** pulls together related ideas, restates suggestions, and offers decisions or conclusions for the group to consider.

6. The **reality tester** makes critical analysis of an idea and tests it against some data to see if it would work.

7. The **procedural technician** records suggestions, distributes materials, and provides other services which enable the group to function.

8. The **energizer** attempts to increase the quality and quantity of task behavior.

9. The **consensus taker** asks to see if a group is nearing a decision and sends up a trial balloon to test a possible conclusion.

Maintenance Role Behaviors. Group *maintenance* roles are types of behavior relevant to the group's remaining in good working order, to having a good climate for task work, and to fostering good relationships that permit maximum use of member resources. Some typical roles of this type are:

1. The **harmonizer** attempts to reconcile disagreements, reduce tension, and get people to explore differences.

2. The **gatekeeper** helps to keep communication channels open, facilitates the participation of others, and suggests procedures that permit sharing remarks. This is especially important for women in mixed sex groups where men usually get two-thirds of the air time, or when the only woman in a group finds herself being ignored.

3. The **encourager** is friendly, warm, and responsive to others and indicates acceptance of others' contributions by facial expressions or remarks.

4. The **compromiser** offers a solution which yields status when his or her own idea or status is involved in a conflict. The compromiser admits error and modifies a suggestion in the interest of group cohesion or growth.

5. The **observer-commentor** comments on and interprets the group's internal process.

6. The **follower** serves as audience and passively goes along with the ideas of others.

The roles in the maintenance behavior category are more stereotyped for women than those in the task category. Since females have traditionally been thought of as expressive, nurturing, supportive, and cooperative, and since men are expected to be more assertive, task oriented, impersonal, and abstract, group members may automatically fall into sex-typed specialties regardless of their personal skills and expertise. It is important to be aware of this stereotype trap and encourage both men and women to freely engage in both task and maintenance roles when appropriate. Consider what usually happens when males and females stick with their more comfortably stereotyped roles.

Female managers with high needs for affiliation assurance are basically concerned with building and maintaining close relationships in the group. On the negative side, this may cause anxiety about hurt feelings through rejection and may even cause them to be jealous and possessive of subordinates. If this pattern develops, it can interfere with objective decision making and affect the quality of its outcome.

If female managers are really concerned about maintaining their well-being, they need to develop their subordinates' potential. At times this requires direct and critical feedback, even if feelings are hurt temporarily. For the good of both the organization and the individual involved, subordinates may have to change their behavior even though they don't want to.

Concern for maintenance behaviors also has a very necessary positive side. Maintenance behaviors help build a climate of openness which enhances communication and builds feelings of security with authority figures. Such "feminine" behaviors as expressing feelings, showing vulnerability, and asking for support are invaluable for building strong collaborative work teams. It seems just as imperative for men to increase their relationship and maintenance behaviors as it is for women to become more assertive and effective in dealing with the realities of power.

Self-Oriented Role Behaviors. The types of behavior which only serve personal objectives at the expense of group task accomplishment and maintenance are *self-oriented* roles. Examples are:

1. The **aggressor** deflates others' status, attacks the group or its values, and jokes in a barbed or semiconcealed way.

2. The **blocker** disagrees and opposes beyond reason, resists stubbornly the group's wish, and uses a hidden agenda to thwart the movement of a group.

3. The **dominator** asserts authority or superiority to manipulate the group or certain group members, interrupts contributions of others, and controls by means of flattery or other forms of patronizing behavior.

4. The **playgirl** makes a display in a flamboyant fashion of her lack of involvement, "abandons" the group while remaining physically with it, and seeks recognition in ways not relevant to the group's task.

5. The **avoider** pursues special interests not related to the group's task, stays off the subject to avoid commitment, and prevents the group from facing up to any controversy.

6. The **help seeker** uses the group to solve personal problems which are unrelated to the group's goals.

In summary, effective groups need to work out an adequate balance of task and maintenance roles. As the group grows and members' needs become integrated with group goals, there will be less self-oriented behavior and more task and maintenance behavior. Effective group members need both the skills in observing what roles are lacking and the flexibility in providing these behaviors when appropriate.

Emotional Issues

There are many forces active in groups that disturb task and maintenance behaviors and contribute to self-oriented behaviors. There are also underlying emotional issues that produce a variety of behaviors which interfere with or are destructive to effective group functioning. These issues cannot be ignored or wished away. Rather, they must be recognized and their causes must be understood. And, as the group develops, conditions must be created that permit these same emotional energies to be channeled in the direction of group effort.

Four primary emotional issues must be dealt with by all members in every group. They concern the four personal problems listed below:

Identity. The questions asked when dealing with the problem of identity are as follows: Why am I here? How am I to present myself to others? What role should I play in the group?

Both the manager and her colleagues anxiously await the outcome of this selection of an appropriate role. In their quest to be taken seriously, many female managers awkwardly attempt to become more like their male colleagues or mentors. Attempting to act against their nature by aggressively taking charge and frequently expressing anger usually causes them to feel more anxious and out of character.[9] Hennig and Jardim have noted that at this point female managers frequently try to recapture their feminine nature by keeping their newly found assertiveness without being oppressive or noncaring.[10]

Control and Power. When tackling the problem of control and power, the questions asked are: Who has the power in the situation? How much power, control, and influence do I have? How much do I need? This is a special dilemma for women who often ignore the presence of power issues in a group. These optimistic women prefer to believe that they are always a part of a team of equals, which most frequently is not the case.

Goals. The questions asked about personal goals are: Can any of my needs be met here? Which of my goals can this group fulfill? To which of the group's goals can I attach myself?

The personal goals which realistically can be achieved depend a lot upon the composition of the group and the nature of its task assignment. Even so, individual objectives concerning increased assertiveness, independence, power, and intimacy are almost always issues to be considered.

Acceptance and Intimacy. When faced with the dual problem of acceptance and intimacy, the questions asked are: Am I accepted by the others? Do I accept them? Do they like me? Do I like them? How close to others do I want to become?

This is usually not a problem in all-male groups where intimacy is automatically avoided. In all-female groups intimacy and openness about relationships are actually the dominant themes. In mixed-sex groups, however, sexual tensions are present and people tend to express concerns about being attracted to the opposite sex.

EMOTIONAL BEHAVIORS AND STYLES

Each of the problems described above create tension and anxiety for the new members of a group. Group members' behavior toward one another will be a product of trying to solve each of these problems and trying to cope with a host of other tensions and anxieties.

Types of Emotional Behavior

Three types of emotional behavior that result from the tension of attempting to resolve these underlying problems are summarized on page 199.

__A Show of Tough Emotions.__ Examples of tough emotions are anger, hostility, and self-assertiveness. These emotions usually have associated behaviors like fighting with others, punishing others, controlling others, or counterdependency. Tough emotions are characteristic of the stereotyped male manager who seems cool, competitive, tough, resilient, and motivated toward task achievement.

__A Show of Tender Emotions.__ Examples of tender emotions are love, sympathy, desire to help, and need for affiliation with others. Symptomatic behaviors of these emotions include supporting and helping others, depending upon others, and pairing up or affiliating with others. Women are traditionally identified with these emotions.

__A Denial of All Emotion.__ The behaviors associated with a denial of all emotion include withdrawing from others and falling back on logic or reason. This is also a stereotyped male response to emotional situations. It is manifested in a logical, problem-solving approach to management and motivated by extrinsic rewards for achievement.

Everyone usually exhibits some degree of each emotional behavior at one time or another. How a manager deals with each behavior depends on what has worked for her in the past and on which emotional style she is most comfortable with.

Types of Emotional Styles

Different people have different styles for reducing tension and expressing emotions. Three "pure types" of emotional styles (see Figure 8-2) are identified and described below.

__The Friendly Helper Style.__ The **friendly helper style** is characterized by an acceptance of tender emotions and a denial of tough emotions. Emotions may be expressed in this style by the following statement, "Let's not fight, let's help each other." Friendly helpers like to give and receive affection but cannot tolerate hostility and fighting. This emotional style is more characteristic of women who have learned to be excessively pleasant, to smooth over conflict, to be overly concerned with having people get along well together (often at the expense of task accomplishment), to smile too much, and to allow themselves to be interrupted. Because of this friendly helper orientation, many female managers abandon positions of strength in order to remain charming and conciliatory.

FIGURE 8-2

TYPES OF EMOTIONAL STYLES

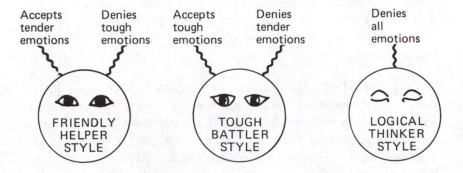

Accepts tender emotions   Denies tough emotions   Accepts tough emotions   Denies tender emotions   Denies all emotions

FRIENDLY HELPER STYLE   TOUGH BATTLER STYLE   LOGICAL THINKER STYLE

The Tough Battler Style. The **tough battler style** is seen in an acceptance of tough emotions and a denial of tender emotions. To express this style, one might say, "Let's fight it out." Tough battlers can deal with hostility but not with love, support, and affiliation, which they see as signs of weakness. This emotional style is often manifested by men who operate more out of a need for power and control than a need to get the job done well. Several very unflattering names exist for women who express their emotions in the tough battler style. Due to traditional social conditioning, few women are oriented in this manner.

The Logical Thinker Style. The **logical thinker style** consists of a denial of all emotion. It is expressed by the following statement: "Let's reason this thing out." Logical thinkers cannot deal with tender or tough emotions. Consequently, they shut their eyes and ears to much of what is going on around them. Based on the conditioning that one should be rational, men typically attempt to exclude needs for closeness and spontaneity to the extent of not even recognizing the emotional content of a message or its relevance to the situation. This is probably the most acceptable mode of dealing with emotions in the rational, male-dominated business world.

In summary, men who behave out of character with their emotional stereotypes are often viewed as "pansies or sissies"; women, as "tomboys or castrating females." These stereotypical expectations need to be broken so that both men and women can be free to express their full range of emotions when appropriate.

Rather than being concerned about whether they are being ignored or deceived, most women need to make their points openly, claim ownership for jobs well done, and acknowledge errors in judgment. Women could benefit from more analytical thinking and healthy assertiveness. Men, on the other hand, need to be more collaborative, less competitive, more open, and less cool in showing their feelings. The male's managerial ability would be enhanced by decreasing exhibitionism and increasing time spent on building support systems.

Whether or not a manager's specific emotional style is appropriate depends on the group situation she is in. All groups need all three styles at one time or another to function effectively. As a good group member, the manager needs to develop emotional flexibility so that she can exhibit the most appropriate emotional behavior when needed.

GROUP STRENGTHS AND WEAKNESSES

The factors just discussed in the previous section are useful in that they help the manager zero in on important aspects of the group process which influence decision-making effectiveness. If she is accurate in her process assessments, she can combine this knowledge with the inherent strengths and weaknesses of groups to manage them effectively.

Advantages of Groups in Decision Making

There are four primary advantages of groups over individuals in decision-making situations which should be capitalized upon.[11] They are discussed on page 202.

1. *Greater amount of knowledge and information.* The sum of the group's knowledge is obviously greater than that of any one individual within it. In addition, different group members are likely to be specialists in different areas so that the combined knowledge is cumulative.

2. *Greater number of approaches.* One reason people have difficulty making decisions by themselves is that they tend to get stuck in ruts or persist in using an unfruitful approach. In groups, the various members have a wider array of approaches to a problem and avoid persisting in a dead-end procedure.

3. *Increased acceptance.* If the manager makes a decision by herself, she must still persuade others to go along with her and implement it. Participation in group decision making increases acceptance because group members share the ownership of whatever decision is reached. It is "our" versus "your" decision.

4. *Better comprehension.* Decisions made by individuals must be communicated to people affected by them. This process carries with it many possibilities of distorting and/or misunderstanding the message. Communication failures are less likely to occur in groups in which all members actively participate in the decision-making process.

Weaknesses of Groups in Decision Making

Groups have many quality and acceptance advantages if their strengths are capitalized on. If they are not managed properly, several weaknesses can hinder the decision-making process.[12] These weaknesses are discussed below.

1. *Social pressure.* This is pressure exerted on group members to conform to the opinion of the majority in order to avoid interpersonal conflicts. The desire to be accepted as one of the gang and not rock the boat has been referred to as "groupthink." This is weakness in decision making because oftentimes better solutions are suppressed in the process.

2. *Momentum.* When a group discusses several alternative solutions to a problem, each alternative receives both supportive and critical comments. It has been shown that the first alternative receiving a positive algebraic sum of 15 tends to be adopted 85% of the time regardless of its quality relative to other alternatives. In other words, after a decision alternative has received 15 more positive comments than negative comments, solutions of higher quality introduced later on have little chance of being adopted.[13]

3. *Individual domination.* In most groups a dominant person emerges; in formal organizations, this person is appointed. While this individual may have more influence on the decision made because of his or her position, persuasive ability, or persistence, actually there is no direct relationship between one's power and the quality of one's decision. A better decision maker may not have enough influence to get alternatives heard by the group.

4. *Winning the argument.* The goal of decision-making groups is to make the best decision for all concerned. Once an individual has expressed preference for one alternative, however, the conflicting secondary goal of winning the argument often emerges. Because of personal ego involvement, the committed person wants to convert others and gain support for a publicly expressed preference. Since winning is not related to the best decision, better ideas that come along later are often sacrificed to feed individual needs to compete and win.

Guidelines for Achieving a Group's Potential

If a group's inherent liabilities can be avoided and its assets capitalized upon, it has the potential in most cases to make better decisions than individuals acting on their own. To achieve the group's potential, the following guidelines are offered:

1. The formal leader should not dominate the meeting but should act as a facilitator.

2. Everyone should avoid evaluating each other's suggestions until all suggestions have been made.

3. Group members should concentrate on their group processes and not just the content of the meeting.

4. Members should listen to understand rather than to refute.

5. Members should be sensitive to the unexpressed feelings of others and act accordingly.

6. The group should be open to minority viewpoints.

CONDUCTING EFFECTIVE MEETINGS

Ask any group member and most will agree that nearly half their time spent in meetings is wasted. If this problem could be even partially corrected, much time could be "recaptured" to be used on more productive tasks. The reader might think back over the last few meetings he or she attended and ask the following questions:

1. Was the meeting necessary?

2. Could the subjects discussed in the meeting have been handled in another manner such as a memo or conference call?

3. Could the meeting have been postponed to a more convenient time for all concerned?

If the reader answered no to the first question and yes to either of the remaining questions, then he or she probably wasted time at that meeting.

Assuming that a meeting is necessary, whether called by a manager or someone else, the manager should follow these guidelines to avoid wasting time and to make meetings more productive:

1. Define the exact purpose of the meeting. Make sure that all who will attend are informed, in advance and in writing, about what is to be discussed at the meeting. This will allow them to come properly prepared.

2. Distribute copies of an agenda for the meeting to all attendees.

3. Limit the time for the meeting. Have a specific starting time and ending time. Remember that work expands to fill the amount of time allotted to it.

4. Choose a good place for the meeting. Proper ventilation, comfort, accessibility, availability of equipment, and so on, are very important.

5. Stick to the items on the agenda. Avoid interruptions and tangential discussions.

6. After the meeting, expedite the preparation and distribution of the minutes of the meeting so that they are in the hands of all attendees no later than two days after the meeting. If any actions are to be taken as a result of the meeting, make sure that everyone knows who is to do what and when.

ACTION GUIDELINES

1. A lone woman in a group tends to withdraw and withhold contributions because she feels isolated and unsupported. This suggests the benefits of placing several women on a team, even if other teams have no women members at all. Providing a "critical mass" also serves to reduce role stereotyping.

2. Analysis of communication patterns in groups can yield important information regarding feelings and influence. Appropriate "gatekeeping" role behavior can help maintain the minority females' influence.

3. Using the consensus decision-making procedure is the best way to assure acceptance of a group decision and to assure that female members have equal input and influence in decisions affecting them.

4. It is important to encourage in groups both task role behaviors and maintenance role behaviors, and to discourage self-oriented role behaviors. Female group

members need to capitalize on the strengths and avoid the weaknesses of their more natural maintenance role behavior, and utilize task roles where appropriate.

5. The emotional issues surrounding identity, power, goals, and intimacy should be aired and talked through rather than suppressed.

6. Both tough and tender emotions are natural and should be expressed at appropriate times in appropriate ways whether one adopts the tough battler, friendly helper, or logical thinker emotional style.

7. Group leaders should capitalize on group decision-making strengths and avoid group weaknesses by acting as facilitators, avoiding premature evaluation of alternatives, concentrating on group process as well as content, and acting in a gatekeeping role.

8. Wasted time in meetings should be avoided by defining the exact purpose of the meeting, distributing an agenda in advance, setting a time limit for the meeting, choosing an appropriate time and place, sticking to the agenda, and promptly distributing written minutes.

FOOTNOTES

1. Margaret Hennig and Anne Jardim, *The Managerial Woman* (New York: Pocket Books, 1978), pp. 196-197.

2. Norma Carr-Ruffino, *The Promotable Woman* (Revised ed.; Belmont, CA: Wadsworth Publishing Co., 1985), pp. 438-440.

3. J. A. F. Stoner, *Management* (2d ed.; Englewood Cliffs, NJ: Prentice-Hall, 1982), pp. 318-319.

4. R. M. Kanter, "On Ending Female Tokenism in T-Groups: Group Norms, Processes, and Sex Role Issues," *Social Change*, Vol. 5, No. 2 (1975), pp. 1-3.

5. A. G. Sargent, "The Androgynous Blend: Best of Both Worlds?" *Management Review* (October, 1978), pp. 60-65.

6. R. M. Kanter, *op. cit.*, p. 3.

7. D. A. Kolb, I. M. Rubin, and J. M. McIntyre, "Group Dynamics," in

Chapter 8, *Organizational Psychology: An Experiential Approach* (Englewood Cliffs, NJ: Prentice-Hall, 1979), pp. 231-249.

8. K. D. Benne and P. Sheats, "Functional Roles of Group Members," *The Journal of Social Issues*, Vol. 4, No. 2 (Spring, 1948), pp. 42-49.

9. A. G. Sargent, *op. cit.*, pp. 62-63.

10. Hennig and Jardim, *op. cit.*, pp. 52-54.

11. N. R. F. Maier, "Assets and Liabilities in Group Problem Solving," *Psychological Review*, 74 (July, 1967), pp. 239-249.

12. *Ibid.*

13. *Ibid.*, p. 242.

CHAPTER 9

Dealing with Difficult Employees

OUTLINE

I. Mismatch of Manager and Employee Behavioral Styles
    A. The Expressive Style
    B. The Driving Style
    C. The Analytical Style
    D. The Amiable Style

II. Personality Problems of Employees
    A. Oversensitive Employees
    B. Hostile or Angry Employees
    C. Negative Employees

III. Signs of Counterproductive Behavior
    A. Disrespect
    B. Lack of Cooperation
    C. Passiveness and Aggressiveness

IV. Approaches to Interpersonal Conflict Situations
    A. Competing
    B. Accommodating
    C. Avoiding
    D. Collaborating
    E. Compromising

V. Prevention of Unnecessary Conflict
    A. Get Initial Agreement
    B. Offer a Limited Choice of Alternatives
    C. Obtain a Commitment in Advance
    D. Communicate Positive Expectations
    E. Use Compliments as Positive Motivators

Action Guidelines

Most managers have some exceptionally good employees and, unfortunately, more than their share of difficult ones. The difficult employees are the ones a manager wants to forget. As hard and as long as she has worked with them, nothing seems to come together. She just can't get on the same wavelength with them.

MISMATCH OF MANAGER AND EMPLOYEE BEHAVIORAL STYLES

Many of a manager's difficult employees may not be that way all the time with all managers. They're difficult only because their behavioral style does not match the manager's behavioral style. That's why other managers with a more compatible behavioral style find it much easier to manage these difficult employees.

A person's behavioral style is his or her habitual way of interacting with another person. Some people, for example, are more assertive, while others are more compliant. *Extroverts* versus *introverts* are terms commonly used to describe people who are more outgoing versus those who are more reserved when interacting with others. People with compatible behavioral styles tend to like each other and naturally get along better than people with incompatible styles. A key managerial skill is knowing how to adapt one's behavioral style so that it is "right" for the difficult employee.

When people act and react, they exhibit behaviors which help define their personality. Research in social psychology shows that there are four distinct behavioral patterns in people.[1] These patterns are the (1) expressive style, (2) driving style, (3) analytical style, and (4) amiable style. Each pattern is described below, along with some specific guidelines a manager can use to change his or her behavioral style to comply with the expectations of each of the four behavioral types among subordinates.

Behavioral style characteristics are especially important when an employee and a manager with incompatible styles come in contact with each other. When that occurs, tension often results. This increased tension usually pushes the employee further away from the manager and makes that person a "difficult" employee. In order to avoid this increased tension, a manager should practice behavioral flexibility: Treat employees the way they want to be treated. Not YOUR way . . . THEIR way!

The Expressive Style

The **Expressives** are animated, intuitive, and lively. But they can also be manipulative, impetuous, and excitable. They are fast paced, make spontaneous decisions, and are not very concerned about facts and details. They thrive on involvement with others.

The Expressives like to interact with other people, so the manager should try not to hurry a discussion with them. She should move at a rapid but entertaining pace. When she finally reaches agreement with an Expressive, she should make sure that both of them fully understand all the details.

The Driving Style

The **Drivers** are firm with others. They are oriented toward productivity and concerned with bottom-line results. But Drivers can be stubborn, impatient, and tough-minded. They like to take control of other people and situations.

The Drivers are easy to deal with as long as the manager is precise, efficient, and well-organized in dealing with them. She should make sure she keeps her relationship businesslike. To influence the Drivers' decisions, the manager should provide options and allow them to draw their own conclusions.

The Analytical Style

The **Analyticals** are persistent, systematic problem solvers. They can also be aloof, picky, and critical. They need to be right—which can lead them to be overreliant on data. Their actions and decisions tend to be extremely cautious and slow.

With the Analytical the manager should try to be systematic, organized, and prepared. Analyticals require solid, tangible, and factual evidence. The manager should take time to list the advantages and disadvantages of any plan she proposes. She should have viable alternatives for dealing with any disadvantages and suggest ways in which the analyticals can take action. However, she should not use any gimmicks to get a fast decision.

The Amiable Style

The **Amiables** are highly responsive, relatively unassertive, supportive, and reliable. However, Amiables are sometimes complaining, softhearted, and acquiescent. They are slow to take action. Before they make a decision, they have to know just how other people feel about the decision. Amiables dislike interpersonal conflict so much that they often tell others what they think others want to hear rather than what is really on their minds.

The manager should try to support the Amiable's feelings. She should show interest in the Amiable as a person. The manager should move along in an informal manner and show the Amiable that she is "actively listening." Both her approach and presentation should be low-key. She should be confident. She should make suggestions and provide personal assurances that any new actions will involve a minimum of risk.

In summary, accepting and understanding that employees are different and need to be managed differently is basic to successful management. If the manager is able to go one step further and identify critical personality traits in her employees, she can manage them the way they would like to be managed. The bottom-line payoff will be greater productivity and more personal satisfaction in all of her relationships with her employees . . . especially the "difficult" employees.

PERSONALITY PROBLEMS OF EMPLOYEES

Of course, there are employees who are difficult to manage for reasons more complicated than differences in behavioral style. Employees with deep-seated personality problems may exhibit work habits, attitudes, and emotional behaviors which reduce their morale and performance, as well as that of their coworkers. Although the manager should leave the solution of such personality problems to psychiatrists or counselors, she should not ignore their existence and the disruption they cause in the workplace. People with personality problems are not easily changed, and disciplinary action is seldom effective. However, there are some positive actions the manager can take to help them.[2]

Oversensitive Employees

Some employees are very sensitive to criticism and are easily hurt. They burst into tears when asked mere information-seeking questions because they assume the manager is dissatisfied with their work. They may also appear unsure of themselves and be reluctant to make suggestions for fear of criticism. With these employees, it is critical to avoid saying anything that will undermine their self-confidence. The manager should praise their work whenever possible and continually reassure them that they are doing a good job. When criticism or productivity problems do arise, she should try to eliminate the personal factor as much as possible by using words like *we* and *our department* when explaining how the work should be improved. Also, she should be careful that these employees don't misinterpret departmental decisions or job assignments as reflections of their capabilities.

Hostile or Angry Employees

Some employees are hard to get along with because they become angry at the slightest provocation. This type of behavior presents a problem not only to the manager, but also to other employees who must work with them. People who continually "fly off the handle" are usually emotionally immature and often have inferiority complexes. Consequently, ordinary disciplinary actions may not work in stemming displays of temper.

Talking constructively with an angry person is usually fruitless. If someone is emotional, the best strategy is to listen, not talk or argue. Angry people are expressing a mixture of feelings that may include resentment, frustration, fear, prejudice, or disappointment, although none of these might be stated directly. The manager should listen to discern what the underlying sources of hostility really are.

The manager shouldn't try to persuade angry employees to

change, nor should she talk to the company counselor on the spot because in the employee's emotional condition, that would only serve as further fuel for the fire. The best she can do, usually, is to assure a hostile employee that she understands that employee's feelings and to show an interest in following up and discussing the problem at a later time when she can check some things out (and the angry employee has had a chance to cool down).

At the later meeting, the hostile employee should be told that the company cannot tolerate such behavior because of its disruptive effects. The manager should not attempt to diagnose the reasons for such behavior herself or even try to correct it. Instead, she should refer the employee to the company counselor or to an outside psychiatrist for evaluation and counseling. If the employee refuses, she must be prepared to inform the employee that such action is mandatory and that refusal will cause him or her to be dismissed from the job.

Negative Employees

Occasionally a manager will run across employees who are by nature pessimistic. They are always thinking of reasons why goals can't be reached, why ideas won't work, and why anything different will not stand a chance. It is difficult to get these employees to be enthusiastic about their work. They give up whenever confronted with a problem of any magnitude whatsoever. Even worse, this gloomy attitude may affect other workers' attitudes.

One thing the manager might try with such employees is a praise-and-compliment strategy. She might accentuate the positive aspects about everything, including the employees, by praising them for their attendance, promptness, or a job well done. This may start a self-fulfilling prophecy of optimism on their part.

If the negative employees give the manager a pessimistic response to a new plan of action, she should demand that they come up with a positive alternative. If they say that something won't work, she should have them come up with something that will. The idea is to jolt the pessimistic employees out of their negative rut. If the manager does this in a positive manner, her own optimistic attitude is apt to make a favorable impression itself.

SIGNS OF COUNTERPRODUCTIVE BEHAVIOR

Difficulties in employee relations do not always arise because of deep-seated personality problems or differences in basic behavioral styles. Sometimes difficulties arise because of employee immaturity or unprofessional attitudes. People in the work environment can be counterproductive for a variety of reasons ranging from lack of understanding to overwhelming personal problems.

There are several psychological techniques that can be used with people who are counterproductive. Some of the techniques can be used in any situation; others assume that one has formal power over the persons involved. Sometimes it is necessary to confront people because of their counterproductive behavior. This technique is not relished by many. It requires tact and confrontation skills. People are not usually amenable to change, rather they resist and fear it. When people are asked to change their behavior, they may become more defensive, angry, and hostile.

From the vantage point of a manager, signs of counterproductive behavior include (1) disrespect, (2) lack of cooperation, and (3) passive and aggressive behaviors. These behaviors are discussed below, along with the techniques that can be used to change them.

Disrespect

A newly appointed female manager should not ignore signs of disrespect from either male or female subordinates because of the possible erosion of her referent power. Although it is common to encounter resistance from male subordinates, she can also meet resistance from other women who feel resentment and inadequacy when they see another woman bypass them in positions of power historically denied to them. Other women's disrespect and negative actions must be dealt with as firmly and directly as male encroachment. When the manager encounters female subordinates acting in negative ways, it sometimes helps to remember that their actions are probably based on naiveté or hurt feelings rather than on maliciousness. In any case it is beneficial to calm herself and practice the techniques of coaching and confronting.

When a female subordinate acts in an unprofessional manner, the manager should call her in and explain the implications the behavior has for the employee's ambitions. The manager should make sure the tone of the discussion is friendly, helpful, and calm rather than threatening or antagonistic. Male supervisors and subordinates expect this kind of coaching, and it is just as crucial to the careers of female supervisors and subordinates.

Lack of Cooperation

Some signs of lack of cooperation include substandard performance or defensive and hostile actions. Look at the following scenario. Anna comes back from lunch on Friday a little giggly and light-headed from her noontime overindulgence. Consequently, she doesn't work effectively for the remainder of the day. This leaves the woman manager with a backlog of work and many errors to be corrected. It is her responsibility to confront Anna with the effect Anna's behavior is having on her.

Although the manager may not enjoy having to deal with the above situation, there are some guidelines for effective confrontation that can help her chances of producing a productive and satisfactory relationship. First of all, she should try to *relax* during the confrontation. If she appears too tense, she may leave the impression that she is not confident. Sometimes a role-playing session or rehearsal will help ease the tension. She should plan carefully what she is going to say so that she doesn't simply fly off the handle and express her frustrations. She may feel better after venting her frustrations, but the problem won't be solved.

A manager will want to vary this technique with the individual and the situation, but she should try to *get to the point* as soon as possible. She shouldn't waste time talking about unimportant issues to ease the tension because the tension is already there!

The manager should *not apologize* or be defensive about the confrontation. This will only weaken her authority. While she wants to be considerate, she must also be firm and uncompromising. She should confront the employee in a nonhostile manner. She can share feelings of anger and frustration productively; but if she is openly hostile, her subordinate's reaction will probably be hostile also. This will lead to a counterproductive outcome.

The manager should *talk about behavior that she notices*, not about inferences that she is gathering from the behavior. For example, she shouldn't tell Anna that something must be bothering her if Anna is drinking too heavily. Rather, she should talk about the behavior she notices. In this case, it is the work that is not being done on Friday afternoons and its consequences.

Many women managers prefer to avoid this type of confrontation in order to prevent any conflict that might ensue. Other women prefer to spend their time in noninfluential roles rather than become involved in power struggles and conflicts. In contrast, men have been taught to overemphasize power and they have been rewarded for doing so. Many even enjoy one-up, one-down interactions even when these are unnecessary or counterproductive.

Many women managers tend to resist taking charge in conflict situations, even when assertive behavior is entirely appropriate. Others actually give away their power or turn to others for help rather than confront the situation themselves.[3] These reactions may be the result of female socialization where women are conditioned to seek help from others rather than be self-reliant. Many women managers have also been socialized to make do with what they have rather than assertively hustle for themselves. These behavior habits result in failures to demand adequate resources for their programs or themselves. To be effective managers, women need to confront conflict situations in the most appropriate manner.

Passiveness and Aggressiveness

Some subordinates want and need to be led, while others seek increased independence and responsibility. It is the manager's responsibility to take the reigns and provide clear directions for those who seek them. She should be careful not to turn over too much of her decision-making power to aggressive subordinates, however, since that may lead to losing part of her legitimate right to have the final say.

The manager *should not expect subordinates to do something because they "ought" to do it*. There will always be genuine differences of opinion about what should be done. The manager should observe her employees closely to learn what incentives there are for them to help her achieve her objectives. One of the most important measures of managerial skill is the ability to persuade people to do things one way in spite of differing opinions.

It is not always a good strategy to be "fair" to subordinates. Being "fair" to a passive person often leads to excessive hand-holding. Being "fair" to an aggressive, manipulative person might enable that person to take over the manager's power and her job. The manager must clearly be in command. If she is not, she may be perceived as weak. Such weakness may produce rivalries and resentments among subordinates who may come to think they are more qualified to handle her position than she is. The manager should be firm, yet courteous, and she'll generate respect and genuine loyalty while keeping hurt feelings to a minimum.

It is necessary to criticize subordinates for their mistakes. Without feedback, a manager's subordinates will not develop an appreciation of what her standards are or learn from their mistakes. It's the way she hands out criticism that's important. Criticism without courtesy can make a passive person feel put down and defensive, or even create the desire for revenge.

It helps to level with subordinates through authentic feedback. **Authentic feedback** consists of nonevaluative interpretations of how a person's or a group's behavior affects one's objectives. It can often lead to increased understanding and decreased resistance to directions when the personal need for feedback is demonstrated and accepted. Sometimes leveling off is done in emotional and evaluative manners. While this type of confrontation is often risky, it is necessary to get feelings out and to open the door to suppressed organizational problems. It is certainly better than suppressing hostile feelings and later transferring them to inappropriate people or circumstances.

Another way to suggest improvements in behavior without bringing out defenses is *to give corrective information in terms of another person or group in a similar situation.* For this tactic to be effective, it is important that the receivers of such information be aware that they are behaving in the same fashion as the other reference person or group. If the awareness is present, indirect comparisons allow the employees to evaluate the manager's suggestions without losing face and becoming defensive.

APPROACHES TO INTERPERSONAL CONFLICT SITUATIONS

In each of the counterproductive situations described above, there was a conflict between the needs of the manager and the employee. **Conflict** is a disagreement between two or more organization members where the concerns of the people involved appear to be incompatible. The main sources of conflict in organizations include the need to share resources, differences in goals, interdependence of work activities, and differences in values or perceptions.

Although some women may have developed a tendency to avoid conflicts earlier in their careers, when they become managers they acquire the responsibility to confront and manage them productively. The specifics of how the manager deals with the person she is in conflict with will depend upon her unique situation and skills. According to Ruble and Thomas, in conflict situations people tend to be primarily concerned with either satisfying their own concerns or cooperating with others to maintain a satisfactory relationship.[4] These two basic dimensions can be combined to define five specific methods of dealing with conflicts (see Figure 9-1). These methods are: (1) competing, (2) accommodating, (3) avoiding, (4) collaborating, and (5) compromising.

After reading the descriptions of common problem-solving approaches given below, the manager may feel that one of these is most characteristic of her. Since none of these approaches is better or worse than any other per se, she should judge the appropriateness of her preferred mode based on how effective it is for the particular situation in which she most frequently finds herself. Some guidelines for when each mode is most appropriate follow the descriptions.

Competing

Competing is assertive and uncooperative behavior where individuals pursue their own concerns at another person's expense. This is often a power-oriented mode of behavior where one uses every technique available to win one's point or defend one's position. This is the stereotypical male response.

Competing is most helpful in situations where quick decisive action is vital, e.g., in emergencies. It is also useful where unpopular courses of action, such as discipline or cost cutting, must be implemented. Finally, competing is a necessary mode of behavior in conflict situations where one must protect oneself against people who

FIGURE 9-1

APPROACHES TO INTERPERSONAL CONFLICT

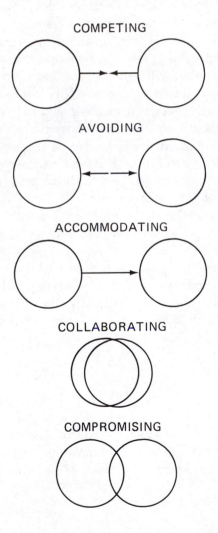

take advantage of noncompetitive behavior. The manager should be careful not to be too competitive, however. If she is, she may find herself surrounded by "yes men" who have learned that it is unwise to disagree with her and, consequently, will close her off from sources of important information.

Accommodating

Accommodating is the opposite of competing. It consists of unassertive and cooperative behavior. Oftentimes the accommodating individual neglects his or her own concerns in order to satisfy the needs of others. Consequently, this appears as a selfless generosity, or a submissive behavior in compliance with another person's wishes. Traditionally, this has been thought of as the more typical feminine response.

Accommodating is a useful strategy for the manager when the issue at stake is much more important to the other person than to her. Satisfying another's needs as a goodwill gesture will help maintain a cooperative relationship. It builds up social credits for later issues and is used appropriately when the manager is concerned about developing subordinates by allowing them to experiment and learn from their own mistakes. She must be careful, however, not to deprive organizational members of her personal contributions or to create a climate where discipline becomes lax.

Avoiding

Avoiding is unassertive and uncooperative behavior where individuals do not pursue either their own concerns or those of others. In avoiding the conflict altogether, a person might diplomatically sidestep an issue, postpone it, or withdraw from the threatening situation. All too often this response is manifested by new female managers who are still uncertain about acting in more assertive manners.

Avoiding is useful when the issue of disagreement is of passing importance or relatively trivial to the manager. Also, if she is in a low-power position or encounters a situation that is very difficult to

change, avoiding may be the best use of her time. This is also true
when the potential damage of confronting a conflict outweighs its
benefits, or when she needs to let people cool off a little in order to
bring tensions back down to a productive level and regain perspective and composure. On the other hand, she should not let important
decisions be made by default or spend a dysfunctional amount of
energy in avoiding issues that eventually must be confronted.

Collaborating

Collaborating is the opposite of avoiding; it consists of assertive and cooperative behavior. It involves an attempt to work with
the other person to find a solution which fully satisfies the concerns
of both parties. This is a joint problem-solving mode involving a lot
of communication and creativity on the part of each party to find a
mutually beneficial solution.

Collaborating is a necessity when an integrative solution is
required in cases where the concerns of both parties are too important to be compromised. Collaborating merges the insights of people
with different perspectives. It allows the manager to test her
assumptions and understanding of others, to gain commitment by
incorporating others' concerns, and to win an opportunity to get rid
of hard feelings. Not all conflict situations, however, deserve this
amount of time and energy. Trivial problems often don't require
optimal solutions, and not all personal differences need to be worked
through. It also does her little good to behave in a collaborative
manner if others do not do the same and take advantage of what she
is trying to accomplish.

Compromising

Compromising falls somewhere between assertive and cooperative behaviors. The objective is to find a mutually acceptable
middle ground which is expedient and partially satisfies both parties. It is manifested by splitting the difference, engaging in concessions, or seeking middle ground positions.

A compromise is useful when goals are moderately important

and not worth the effort of collaboration or the possible disruption of competition. If the manager is dealing with an opponent of equal power who is strongly committed to a mutually exclusive goal, compromise may be the best hope for leaving both of them in relatively satisfactory positions. The same would be true if there were a high degree of time pressure and she needed to achieve a temporary settlement very quickly. Compromise is a useful safety valve for gracefully getting out of mutually destructive situations. On the other hand, it is possible to concentrate on compromise so heavily that the manager can lose sight of more important principles, values, and long-term objectives. Too much compromise can also create a cynical climate of gamesmanship.

PREVENTION OF UNNECESSARY CONFLICT

Some conflict is beneficial because it opens up new alternatives and improved ways of doing things. Other conflict is destructive, especially that which is generated from personality problems or counterproductive attitudes. There are some things which the manager can do, however, to prevent negative conflict from ever getting started.

Get Initial Agreement

The manager should get an initial agreement with persons or groups who object to her attempts at wielding influence. This is important to insure that she is not turned off by them immediately. Showing that she has something in common with them serves to favorably dispose them to both herself and her request by building referent power. If she contradicts herself later on, or proposes contrary approaches, they are more apt to be open to her and her ideas if they believe that she is similar to them.

Offer a Limited Choice of Alternatives

People like to feel that they have some power over what happens to them. But when they are faced with an unlimited number of alternatives to choose from, it is very difficult to make a decision. The strategy of providing a limited choice maximizes the manager's chances of having others accept a request she makes because it lets them make a choice, but only from alternatives acceptable to her. The key is to phrase her questions as if a given event will take place and that others would have to choose how or when this event will take place. When a person is confronted with a limited choice of alternatives and asked to choose from them, most often he or she will do so. And only rarely will this person question initial assumptions or raise additional alternatives.

Compare the following approach, "Can we get together sometime to discuss ways of improving this situation?" with one which says, "I've arranged to have the conference room available on either Monday or Friday afternoon to discuss how we can change this situation. Which day do you prefer?"

Obtain a Commitment in Advance

Obtaining a commitment in advance creates an obligation to implement something later. The advantages and disadvantages of a commitment become more prominent at different times. The advantages are clearer when the event is to take place in the distant future. As the event becomes more immediate, however, the disadvantages become more eminent. Since most people feel compelled to meet their obligations, it is to the manager's advantage to gain a commitment to participate in an activity well in advance of its planned occurrence. If participants feel that they have made a prior commitment, they will find it more difficult to back out when the anxieties associated with the approach of the event occur.

Communicate Positive Expectations

Communicating positive expectations fosters success. Indicating to a person that he or she is expected to be a valuable participant can often act as a self-fulfilling prophecy. That is, he or she will behave in such a way that the manager's expectations will be fulfilled in order for the person to prove worthy of the manager's high regard. Successful use of this approach also decreases begrudging participation because employees feel that they are important and are doing something valuable for the manager—which they are.

Use Compliments as Positive Motivators

Compliments are positive motivators. Trying to get someone to act through criticism has negative consequences even if the strategy produces results. People usually take criticism as a slap in the face and react defensively and with hostility toward its source. The manager should phrase her criticism in positive terms and frost it with preceding compliments. For example, a line manager could say to a staff group leader, "We like your work very much. If your people would take a little more interest in personally relating your ideas with ours, we could probably make even better use of them." Compare this statement with, "Your people think they are such experts that they won't even come down off their high horse to relate as human beings so that we can understand what they're talking about."

ACTION GUIDELINES

Dealing with difficult employees is inevitable. A manager's effectiveness in turning around a potentially counterproductive situation depends upon her abilities to correctly diagnose what is going on, to discern the appropriate corrective behavior, and to implement that behavior effectively. The following guidelines summarize the appropriate actions to take after she has confronted a difficult situation:

1. When the manager encounters a behavioral style mismatch, she should first determine her subordinate's style and then behave so as to decrease tension and build trust. With Expressives, she shouldn't hurry; she should be entertaining and check the details of any agreements. With Drivers, she should be precise, efficient, well organized, and businesslike. With Analyticals, she should be systematic, organized, prepared, and factual. With Amiables, she should show personal interest and be more informal.

2. When dealing with employees who have personality problems, the manager should leave the solution of their personal difficulties to a qualified psychiatrist or psychologist. She should avoid disruptions and keep the subordinates productive and at work. With oversensitive employees, she should avoid undermining their self-confidence and try to praise and reassure them as much as possible. With hostile employees, she should listen for the underlying source of frustration and set up a later meeting, when feelings have cooled down, to explain the guidelines for acceptable behavior and to refer the employee for counseling. With negative employees, she should attempt to reverse their attitudes with a praise-and-compliment strategy, and always emphasize the positive.

3. When the manager encounters unprofessional attitudes or behavior in subordinates, she can't afford to ignore them because of possible erosion of her managerial power base. If a subordinate treats her with disrespect, she should explain the implications of these actions in a calm, professional way. When confronting a subordinate about counterproductive behavior, she should not apologize; she should get to the point as quickly as possible, making sure that she discusses actual behavior rather than inferences regarding its source. She shouldn't expect employees to do something because they "ought" to do it. She should be firm, yet courteous, when giving them directions. When it is necessary to criticize subordinates for mistakes, she should use authentic feedback and indirect comparisons to allow them to evaluate her suggestions without losing face and becoming defensive.

4. In conflict situations, the manager should react in the manner most appropriate for the situation. She should: *compete* in emergency situations where quick decisive action is necessary; *accommodate* when the issue at stake is much more important to the other person than to her and when she wants to build goodwill; *avoid* when the issue of disagreement is trivial to her or when the potential damage of the conflict outweighs the benefits; *collaborate* when an integrative solution is required to meet two equally important opposing needs; and *compromise* when goals are moderately important and not worth the effort of collaboration to escape a mutually destructive situation or to meet time deadlines.

5. The manager should prevent unnecessary conflicts by using the strategies of getting initial agreement, offering a limited choice of alternatives, obtaining a commitment in advance, communicating positive expectations, and using compliments as positive motivators.

FOOTNOTES

1. P. Hunsaker and A. J. Alessandra, *The Art of Managing People* (Englewood Cliffs, NJ: Prentice-Hall, 1980).

2. W. H. Weiss, "Supervising Employees with Personality Problems," *Supervisory Management*, 28, 2 (February, 1983), pp. 8-13.

3. A. G. Sargent, "The Androgynous Blend: Best of Both Worlds," *Management Review* (October, 1978), pp. 60-65.

4. T. L. Ruble and K. W. Thomas, "Support for a Two-Dimensional Model of Conflict Behavior," *Organizational Behavior and Human Performance*, 16 (1976), pp. 143-155.

CHAPTER 10

Hiring and Firing Employees

OUTLINE

I. Recruiting Employees
    A.   Job Analysis
    B.   Recruitment Sources

II. Screening the Applications

III. The Selection Interview
    A.   Interviewing Candidates
    B.   Good Questions
    C.   Ambiguous Questions
    D.   Poor Questions

IV. The Hiring Decision
    A.   Importance of the Background Check
    B.   Methods of Checking References

V. Firing Employees

VI. A Final Note

Two of the most important responsibilities of managers are selecting and discharging their employees—responsibilities that are associated with the management function of staffing. More than anything else, employee selection should be seen as a *matching process*. How well an employee is matched to a job affects the quantity and quality of the employee's work (as well as the manager's subsequent work!). Workers who are unable to produce the expected quantity and quality of work can cost an organization money, time, and trouble. This chapter will be concerned with the hiring and firing of employees.

RECRUITING EMPLOYEES

In recruiting future employees, most organizations divide their recruiting function into at least two types. First, the organization uses a process called *general recruiting* for low-level positions. This is a continual process which is directed at filling positions that frequently open up in most organizations. Examples of low-level positions include those for various clerical work, janitorial work, and other unskilled or semiskilled work. To fill higher level positions, an organization may opt for *specific recruiting*. This process is most appropriate for recruiting professional employees who are needed to do a specific or unique job.

For both general recruiting and specific recruiting, two issues are important to consider: job analysis and the sources of recruitment.

Job Analysis

Before managers can recruit personnel, they must know what type of position is open. This is the purpose of job analysis.[1] **Job analysis** consists of a statement that depicts the following: (1) a description that identifies the title, duties, and responsibilities for that position; and (2) an acknowledgment of the desired background, experience, and personal characteristics an individual must have in order to perform effectively in the position. For example, an open position for an auditing manager in an accounting firm may state: "Position requires a BA or MS in accounting, CPA, minimum five years experience, some experience as a supervisor, and good interpersonal skills."

Recruitment Sources

Two main sources of recruitment can be used by managers: internal and external. The **internal recruitment sources** are those tapped within the organization. These may be existing employees or employee referrals (employees' friends). The recruiting is initiated by means of job posting within the organization's premises. Many organizations find it useful to recruit or promote existing employees to open positions because (1) it significantly reduces recruiting and placement costs, and (2) it fosters improved morale and loyalty among employees because they believe that consistently good performance will be rewarded with a promotion.[2]

External recruitment sources are also frequently used by organizations. They include walk-in applicants, placement/search firms, newspaper ads, college placement offices, unions, military services, and professional associations. The vast variety of external sources available will almost ensure that the organization will be able to find an adequate number of candidates. On the negative side, utilizing external sources can take a lot of time. Most organizations must interview between 20 and 30 candidates before one is hired. Newspaper ads also can be expensive, as is using a placement firm for more specialized or high-level managerial positions.

The growing body of research that has investigated the relationship between recruiting source and rates of turnover has yielded surprisingly consistent results.[3] These studies indicate that internal sources, particularly employee referrals, were consistently good sources of personnel who remained in the organization for a significant length of time. Employment agencies, on the other hand, were poor sources of long-term employees.

SCREENING THE APPLICATIONS

Once a position has been advertised, the manager of the unit for which it has to be filled may be inundated by resumes and letters of application. Many people may even call the manager directly about the position.

Certain steps are taken to process applications for jobs in most organizations. Variations on this basic progression depend upon organizational differences, including factors such as the size of the organization, nature of the jobs to be filled, number of people to be selected, and pressure of outside factors such as equal employment opportunity considerations.

In some organizations selection activities, such as screening initial applications, may be centralized into a specialized unit within the personnel department. In others, the screening may be performed by the manager of the unit for which the position is to be filled. Regardless of who screens the initial applications, the emphasis should be on narrowing the pool of applicants generated by the recruiting activities to a select few. The emphasis should be on trying to match the best available persons with the jobs to be filled. These persons should be invited for a formal interview.

THE SELECTION INTERVIEW

The formal interview of candidates is the most important step in hiring employees for two major reasons. First, it provides a great variety and volume of information about the candidate (for the organization), as well as about the organization (for the candidate). Second, the candidate's meeting face to face with many organizational members is invaluable in determining the degree of fit or match with the organization's needs.

There are three general types of interviews that are most frequently used: structured, semistructured, and unstructured. In the **structured interview**, the interviewer prepares a list of questions in advance and does not deviate from the list. This type of interview allows an interviewer to prepare questions which are job related, and then to complete a standardized evaluation. Companies under heavy pressure from the EEOC often use the structured interview because it provides documentation in the event that anyone questions why one applicant was hired instead of another. The structured interview might also be used when time pressures are present or when many candidates are being interviewed.

The **semistructured interview** consists of a limited set of prepared questions that are asked of the candidate. This type of interview is used when there are few candidates to interview. Also, it allows for more flexibility than the structured interview.

Finally, in the **unstructured interview** little preparation other than a set of example topics is made. In this type of interview, the interviewer may ask general questions to prompt the applicant to discuss herself or himself. The interviewer then uses the applicant's responses to shape the next question. For example, if the applicant says, "I really enjoyed working with my manager at my previous job," the interviewer might then ask, "What type of manager do you most enjoy working with?"

While the interviewer/manager wants to gain as much information as possible from the candidate, there are limitations that have been imposed as a result of antidiscrimination laws. Many questions that appear to be harmless can be construed as discriminatory in selection decisions. The important criterion is that, unless a question relates directly to the job or to specific needs, it normally cannot be asked. Many experts feel that the safest and fairest type of interview to use is the structured interview.[4]

Interviewing Candidates

Many people think the ability to interview a person is an innate talent. Just because an individual is personable and likes to talk is no guarantee that this person will be a good interviewer. The questioning techniques used by an interviewer can significantly affect the type and quality of information obtained.

Figure 10-1 is a guide which could be used by firms in interviewing applicants for sales jobs. It identifies the questions that the interviewer is to ask of the job applicant and explains what the questions are probing for. Of course, the answer given by the job applicant is assessed by the interviewer in light of what the interviewer wants in a candidate for that specific position. Obviously the questions that would be asked of someone applying for a data processor's job would be different from those asked of someone applying for a salesperson's job. The purpose behind any effective employment interviewing is the same: to ask questions and find out if the person being interviewed will or will not make a good employee.

FIGURE 10-1

GUIDE TO IMPROVE EMPLOYMENT INTERVIEWING FOR SALES-RELATED JOBS

<u>Question</u>

<u>Purpose of Question</u>

1. Why are you interested in a job with _____?

The interviewer should find out in detail what the candidate knows about the company's growth, product lines, pricing, quality, and service. How much research has the applicant done to sell himself or herself or to be familiar with the product he or she knows best? This is a good indicator of how the applicant would approach the selling of products.

2. What did you accomplish in your last job that you were most proud of?

Here the interviewer is looking for the applicant's real depth. The interviewer should listen for the applicant's figures, volumes, number of accounts opened, growth of his or her territory, increased profitability, etc., and make notes to verify the given information at a later date. The interviewer can get a good insight into the applicant from the value the applicant attaches to his or her accomplishments.

3. How did you get your previous jobs?

This question provides a good look into the applicant's resourcefulness. If the applicant obtained past jobs by setting out on a definite campaign to obtain them, then this type of resourcefulness and imagination may be valuable to the organization.

4. Which of your previous jobs did you like best and which least?

The interviewer should insist on specifics in the answer to this question! Was it the boss, the travel, the compensation plan, the product line, the territory, the opportunity, or some other element? The interviewer should keep coming back with a questioning "why?" It is normal to have preferences. Direct answers to these questions can give the interviewer specific information as to how the applicant will fit into the job for which he or she is being considered.

FIGURE 10-1 (Continued)

Question	Purpose of Question
5. (a) What is the major asset that you can bring to _____?	Here is where the interviewer can learn about the applicant's confidence. Does the applicant really believe in himself or herself—or in the products he or she sells? If the applicant doesn't, no one else will!
5. (b) What are your major weaknesses?	The person who is aware of his or her faults can make an honest effort to correct them and, equally important, show insight and thought in evaluating his or her own situation. The applicant who candidly states that he or she has no faults is turning on the caution light—this should be followed up with straightforward, very direct questioning!

Good Questions

The questioning techniques used in an interview significantly affect the type and quality of information obtained. Some types of questions provide more meaningful answers than others. Good interviewing techniques are dependent upon the use of open-ended questions directed toward a particular goal. An open-ended question is one that cannot be answered with a yes or no. *Who, what, when, why, tell me, how, which* are all good ways to begin questions that will produce longer, more meaningful, and informative answers. For example, "What was your attendance record on your last job?" is a better question than "Did you have a good attendance record on your last job?" The latter question can be answered with a simple yes or no.

The following is a list of 25 suggested questions which can elicit valuable information from an interviewee:

1. What type of job are you most interested in?

2. Why do you think you might like to work for our organization?

3. What jobs have you held in the past? How were they obtained, and why did you leave?

4. Why did you choose your particular field of work?

5. What do you know about our organization?

6. Why do you feel that you have received a good general education?

7. What qualifications do you have that make you feel that you will be successful in your field? How do they relate to the job for which you are applying?

8. What personal characteristics are necessary for success in your chosen field? ·

9. Why do you think you would like this particular job?

10. Do you prefer to work with others or by yourself?

11. What kind of boss do you prefer? Why?

12. What have you learned from your previous jobs that might help you in the position you are applying for?

13. What interests you in our organization?

14. What do you know about opportunities in the field in which you are trained?

15. During which hours of the day do you do your best work? Would you be willing to work at night?

16. What job in our organization would you choose if you were entirely free to do so? Why?

17. What jobs have you enjoyed the most? the least? Why?

18. What position in our organization do you wish to work toward? Why?

19. What have you done that demonstrates initiative and a willingness to work? Why do you say so?

20. How do you get along with your family and friends? Are they important to you? Why?

21. What is your major weakness? Why do you consider it a weakness?

22. Would you say you have an analytical mind, or are you more creative? What evidence do you have of this ability?

23. What are your unique talents or abilities?

24. What course in school did you like the best and why?

25. What course did you like least? Why?

Ambiguous Questions

Many of the questions below appear rather ambiguous on the surface. Immediately after each question is a parenthetical translation of these seemingly ambiguous questions.[5]

1. *Will you tell me a little bit about yourself?* Translates to: How much trouble have you taken to progress in your career? How well are you able to track your professional life?

2. *Why do you want to leave your current employer?* Translates to: What is the nature of your dissatisfactions and how rationally and coherently are you able to express them?

3. *Will you tell me some things about your current job?* Translates to: Give me a concisely expressed summary of your present responsibilities in a way that enables me to see how well your current work will have applications here.

4. *What do you think of your current management?* Translates to: To what extent are your present dissatisfactions likely to be duplicated here?

Poor Questions

The skillful interviewer will ask pertinent questions and glean much information from the applicant. However, certain kinds of questions should be avoided. Some of these poor questions are:

1. *Questions that rarely produce a true answer.* An example is "How did you get along with your coworkers?" This question is almost inevitably going to be answered with, "Just fine." Most job applicants are on good behavior and are not likely to reveal their weaknesses.

2. *Leading questions.* A leading question is one in which the answer is obvious from the way the question is asked. For example, when interviewing a person who is expected to have a good deal of public contact, the response to "You do like to talk to people, don't you?" will be "Of course."

3. *Illegal questions.* Questions eliciting information about race, creed, sex, age, national origin, marital status, number of children, and so on, are illegal.

4. *Obvious questions.* An obvious question is one for which the interviewer already has the answer (from the completed application form), and the applicant knows it. Questions already answered on the application blank should be probed, not asked again. If an interviewer asks, "What high school did you attend?", the applicant is likely to answer, "As I wrote on my application form, South High School in Milwaukee." Instead, the interviewer should ask questions that probe the information given such as, "What were your favorite subjects at South High, and why were they your favorite?"

5. *Questions that are not job related.* All questions asked should be directly related to the job for which the applicant has applied. Some people believe that a discussion about the weather, sports, or politics helps an applicant to relax. However, those questions consume interview time that could be more appropriately used in other ways. Also, many times the applicant does not relax; and the interviewer may not

listen to the responses because he or she is using the "chit-chat" time to review the candidate's application form or to otherwise make up for his or her lack of planning and preparation.

THE HIRING DECISION

Once the steps of recruiting, screening the applications, and interviewing are completed, the manager may be ready to make the job offer. At this point a background check is usually made.

Importance of the Background Check

The **background check** consists of verifying information obtained from the candidate and collecting additional references. An important group of references is the applicant's previous employers. It is important for the interviewer/manager to remember, however, that under the Fair Credit and Reporting Act, a prospective employer is required to secure the applicant's permission before checking references about the applicant's financial situation.[6]

A manager for a large petrochemical company had this to say about reference checks:

> Unless you do your homework on reference checks, you may end up with good friends, relatives, and old cronies telling you that the candidate is able to do everything, including the ability to leap over tall buildings. I ask the applicant to provide me with the names of the harshest judges of his or her performance. I also like to check back over two previous employers.

Methods of Checking References

Several methods of obtaining information from references are available. Telephoning a reference is the most widely used and preferred method because people are often hesitant to put negative information in writing. Most of the other methods are written ones. Some firms have preprinted reference forms that are sent to individuals who are acting as references for applicants. Specific or general letters of reference are requested by some employers and/or provided by applicants.[7]

FIRING EMPLOYEES

When an employeee is not able to perform adequately on a job, he or she may be discharged, or fired. Without a doubt, one of the most painful managerial tasks is to make the following statement to a subordinate:

"You're fired."

It is rarely said that way anymore. Today a more humanistic vocabulary exists, and a termination interview allows for more empathy. Yet, no matter what is said, the ultimate message is: You're fired, rejected, and unemployed.

Firing is the most drastic disciplinary action that a manager can take. It is done only for the most serious offenses. Altercations, theft, gambling, insubordination, and inability to perform the job are the most common reasons for firing employees.

When an employee is discharged, he or she loses all seniority standing and privileges. Since firing is such a drastic form of termination, careful documentation and consideration of the events justifying the discharge should be done by the manager.

It is often impossible to fire unionized workers in some organizations because of seniority rules, union-management contractual agreements, a limited supply of replacements, or the overall philosophy of the organization. In general, managers are reluctant to discharge employees. Managers often spend a great deal of energy rationalizing and procrastinating when making the decision to fire a subordinate. However, if a manager doesn't fire a problem employee, the manager is likely to become part of the problem also. According to Oberle:

Failure to administer disciplinary actions can result in implied acceptance or approval. Thereafter, problems may become more frequent or severe . . . and ultimately the supervisor will become ineffective in performing one of the primary responsibilities associated with such a position.[8]

If a manager, after carefully considering all factors, finds it necessary to fire an employee, he or she might follow the guidelines presented below to avoid becoming part of the problem:

1. *Tell the employee why.* The basic requirements for firing are simple. The subordinate being fired must be told plainly that he or she has to leave the company. The employee also must be told why. It is important to explain the dismissal in a way that allows employees to preserve self-esteem and to explain to their friends and family why they were fired. But the use of tact in explaining should not be allowed to obscure the realities about an employee's infraction or inadequate performance.

2. *Tell the employee yourself.* In addition to telling the subordinate clearly that he or she is terminated, a manager should undertake the firing of his or her direct subordinates. Delegating the job to someone who doesn't know the situation in detail is not fair to the employee being fired. At the same time, delegating the task of firing may give the employee an opportunity to muddy the issue by developing arguments about the merits of the case.

3. *Other matters.* The employee who is being fired is entitled to know about a number of matters that are inevitably of some concern. One matter involves the way any announcement of the employee's departure from the company will be made, and to what the departure will be attributed. The high-level employee will certainly want to know how much time is left and whether, in the interim, he or she can use the office to arrange to have telephone messages taken. Also, the employee will want to know where the manager stands on providing future references.

A FINAL NOTE

The importance of staffing cannot be overemphasized. An organization needs people. Without human resources there is no organization. Each person making up the human resource must be attracted to the organization. It is the staffing process through which attempts are made to match jobs with people. The better the match, the better the performance of the organization, and the easier the manager's job!

FOOTNOTES

1. Andrew D. Szuilazyi, Jr., *Management and Performance* (Santa Monica, CA: Goodyear Publishing Co., 1981), p. 336.

2. *Ibid.*, p. 337.

3. P. J. Decker and E. T. Cornelius, "A Note on Recruiting Sources and Job Survival Rates," *Journal of Applied Psychology* (August, 1979), pp. 463-464.

4. R. Cochran, J. Cochran, and M. Jennings, "Legal Restrictions in Interviewing and Hiring," *Journal of Accountancy* (September, 1982), p. 41.

5. S. Landau and G. Bailey, "What Every Woman Should Know," *Organizational Reality: Reports from the Firing Line*, edited by P. Frost, V. Mitchell, and W. Nord (Glenview, IL: Scott, Foresman and Company, 1982), p. 15.

6. Robert Mathis and John Jackson, *Personnel: Human Resource Management*, (4th ed.; St. Paul, MN: West Publishing Co., 1985), p. 263.

7. D. B. Wonder and Kenneth S. Kelemen, "Increasing the Value of Reference Information," *Personnel Administrator* (March, 1984), pp. 98-103.

8. R. Oberle, "Administering Disciplinary Actions," *Personnel Journal* (January, 1978), p. 57.

Changing for Success

OUTLINE

I. Strategies for Handling Conflicts in a Managerial Setting
   A. Changing the Other Person
   B. Changing the Situation
   C. Changing Oneself

II. Practical Tips on Changing Oneself

III. Evaluation of the Manager's Skills
   A. Pursuing a Managerial Career
   B. Assuming a Managerial Job
   C. Projecting a Good Image
   D. Finding Mentors
   E. Managing Oneself
   F. Developing Effective Communication Skills
   G. Handling Power and Politics
   H. Working Effectively with Groups
   I. Dealing with Difficult Employees
   J. Hiring and Firing Employees

IV. A Plan to Follow
   A. Becoming Aware of the Need for Change
   B. Having the Willingness and Desire to Change
   C. Acquiring the Knowledge One Needs to Change
   D. Reinforcing One's New Behavior

V. Conclusion

Most of what a manager should have learned so far from this book will transfer to her work situation. This final chapter is designed to (1) give her guidance in handling conflicts on the job, (2) offer practical tips on successfully changing herself, (3) help her evaluate herself on the skills that have been discussed in each of the previous ten chapters, and (4) provide her with a plan for success.

STRATEGIES FOR HANDLING CONFLICTS IN A MANAGERIAL SETTING

Whenever a manager encounters conflict, she generally has three ways of handling the situation. She can try to change either the other person, the situation, or herself. All three strategies may be appropriate at any given time.

Changing the Other Person

The typical response to a managerial conflict with another person is to try to change that person. How often has one heard, "If only her attitude would change ..." or "If only he would see things my way." It is very tempting to believe that a problem in management lies entirely with the other person. In that way the manager doesn't have to look at her own behavior or accept any responsibility for being part of the problem. Yet, when she insists on changing that person to suit her values, attitudes, or needs, it becomes very hard to maintain good human relationships with that person. That person will resent the manager's attitude that only the other has a problem. Remember that part of a manager's job is to effectively manage human resources. In several chapters of this book, we have shown how the manager can help a person change, grow, or be positively motivated through the effective use of managerial skills.

Changing the Situation

There may be times when a difficult relationship at work simply cannot be resolved despite all the manager does to make a go of it. In these cases it may be better for her to transfer to another department or try another company. However, the decision to withdraw from a situation is the most difficult to make. It involves giving up a known situation for something that is unknown. The risk often seems higher than it really is.

It may be necessary for the manager to take legal action if she is the victim of sex discrimination. Chapter 5 on "Managing Yourself" gave information to aid in diagnosing this situation. However, she needs to be aware of the trap of changing her situation to avoid confronting her own shortcomings and accepting responsibility for her behavior.

Changing Oneself

This book has reinforced the concept that one can be in control of one's own behavior—from making the transition to a managerial job to projecting the right image and to managing and communicating with other people. The woman manager is ultimately responsible for herself.

Changing oneself is a logical, intelligent approach to many managerial problems. The manager should accept responsibility for her actions, feelings, and attitudes. No matter how realistic her desire to change is, however, it remains no more than wishful thinking until she develops a plan or contract to achieve her goals. The contract she makes with herself will translate her desire to change into determining *how* she will bring about these changes. By establishing a contract with herself, she is tapping her potential and increasing her ability to achieve her personal and career goals. In addition, her changed behavior may even cause other people to decide that they, too, will change.

PRACTICAL TIPS ON CHANGING ONESELF

With the guidance offered in this section, the manager can put into action specific techniques to modify her behavior. It will take some planning and effort on her part, but real change and growth is possible.

Sperry, Mickelson, and Hunsaker offer the following specific practical tips for being successful in changing oneself:[1]

1. *Be open to new ideas*. As the manager begins to change her behavior, she may notice that people are responding to her differently. She may be getting feedback that is new to her. She should be open to it and should not make judgments for awhile. She should let the new ideas and responses come in and work themselves out.

2. *Use fantasy to predict success*. If a manager has ever participated in sports, she has probably fantasized herself as the victor. For example, prior to the racquetball or tennis game she played, she may have visualized how she would hit the ball, what strategy she would use to defeat her opponent, and so forth. The same process can be used when she begins her self-change program. She imagines what hurdles she will face, how she can overcome them, where the challenges will come from, and what she will be like when she completes her change.

3. *Expect success*. When a manager expects success, she has a better chance of achieving it. Expecting success can help her to take advantage of the self-fulfilling prophecy we have talked about in this book. If she can dream it and plan it, then she can do it!

4. *Maintain some anchor points*. The manager should try to keep some points stable when she is in the midst of making changes. She should keep her attention on her self-change program and not attempt to make too many changes too fast.

5. *Be patient*. Change is a process. Growth occurs over time and in a gradual fashion. The techniques for change are only tools. These tools interact with a manager's behavior and the behavior of others. Over a period of time, changes will occur. Some of the changes may be different from what she expected.

6. *Solicit feedback and advice from others.* Feedback and advice, especially from "disinterested" parties, can provide a fresh perspective on how the manager is doing. Feedback and advice from such persons are critical in helping her to assess the success of her change efforts.

EVALUATION OF THE MANAGER'S SKILLS

Assessing one's skills and abilities is the first essential step in any change strategy. Self-assessment means evaluating one's strengths and weaknesses, as well as one's potential for improvement. In this section we will review briefly the various principles discussed in each of the previous ten chapters and then present self-assessment continuums which are designed to help the manager determine her strengths and weaknesses in these areas. If she finds herself low in any areas on a continuum, she will want to work on improving her skills in those areas.

One of the objectives of this type of evaluation is to provide a long-term, progressive assessment of one's skills. The manager should do the assessment now. Then, in about four to six months, we suggest she go through the continuums again. She might want to mark any change in her behavior with a different colored marker or pencil. Throughout the years of her career, she can return to these continuums, each time measuring her progress.

Pursuing a Managerial Career

In Chapter 1 we discussed special problems for women who are making the transition to a managerial career. When a woman chooses to make a career in management, she must overcome three barriers to success: her traditional upbringing, the attitudes of her male and female colleagues, and the lack of support systems to help her stay in her job.

FIGURE 11-1

DO I RECOGNIZE THE BARRIERS WOMEN FACE IN PURSUING A MANAGERIAL CAREER?

| I am very weak in this area | I am somewhat weak in this area | I am strong in this area | I am very strong in this area |

Note: On this and all other continuums presented in this chapter, the manager should place an *X* on the horizontal line to indicate at which point on the continuum she rates herself.

Fortunately many men and women are breaking out of these traditional roles. Over the past few years women have entered business in increasing numbers and in professions previously considered to be the male domain. Women also have a wider variety of options available than ever before. Many women are rejecting the old image of females as passive, illogical, dependent, and totally supportive of others. Many men are choosing new roles, too. They are working hard to dispel the "John Wayne" myth that men must always be in control, emotionally unexpressive, logical, and achievement oriented. They realize that the rigid male role has had devastating effects on men's health and on their relationships with women and other men.

Despite these changes, sexist attitudes will be a part of everyday life for many years to come. The woman manager will need to develop skills in order to handle sexist behavior in a calm, nonthreatening manner.

FIGURE 11-2

HOW SKILLED AM I IN USING HUMAN RELATIONS TECHNIQUES TO DEAL WITH SEXIST BEHAVIOR IN A MANNER THAT PRESERVES THE INTEGRITY OF BOTH SEXES?

| I am very weak in this area | I am somewhat weak in this area | I am strong in this area | I am very strong in this area |

Developing skills to deal with sexism can be extremely valuable in today's business world. The manager should try to avoid a "men versus women" attitude. If she feels she needs to work on these skills, she might consult the list of suggested readings at the end of this book. She should remember that she is trying to overcome deeply ingrained attitudes toward the "appropriate" roles for men and women in order to view men and women as professional colleagues.

Assuming a Managerial Job

The manager's job entails the critical skills of planning, organizing, staffing, leading, and controlling. A self-assessment of these critical managerial skills should be done periodically. Candid assessment can help the manager formulate her plans for self-improvement.

FIGURE 11-3

HOW ARE MY PLANNING SKILLS?

Do I:
- Assess and establish priorities?
- Have realistic short- and long-range plans?
- Set realistic timetables?

I am very weak in this area	I am somewhat weak in this area	I am strong in this area	I am very strong in this area

FIGURE 11-4

HOW ARE MY ORGANIZING SKILLS?

Do I:
- Make optimal use of personnel and material resources to achieve goals?
- Clearly define responsibilities for subordinates?
- Minimize confusion and inefficiency?

I am very weak in this area	I am somewhat weak in this area	I am strong in this area	I am very strong in this area

FIGURE 11-5

HOW ARE MY CONTROLLING SKILLS?

Do I: • Establish appropriate procedures to be kept informed of my subordinates' work progress?
        • Identify deviations in work-goal progress?
        • Make adjustments to insure that established goals are met?

I am very weak in this area	I am somewhat weak in this area	I am strong in this area	I am very strong in this area

If the manager finds herself needing improvement in basic management skills, she may want to consult some of the basic management texts listed in the suggested readings. Going back to school, attending speeches and training events, or joining professional groups are other ways she may choose to improve herself in this area.

Projecting a Good Image

Impressions develop quickly in a business setting. Within a few seconds the person a manager has contact with may feel threatened, offended, or comfortable. Although making a first impression is challenging, the manager can control the impression she makes on others. The image she projects is formed by a variety of factors including dress, tone of voice, personal mannerisms, facial expressions, hair style, and handshake.

FIGURE 11-6

DO I PROJECT THE TYPE OF IMAGE THAT WILL CREATE POSITIVE FIRST IMPRESSIONS IN A BUSINESS SETTING?

I am very weak in this area	I am somewhat weak in this area	I am strong in this area	I am very strong in this area

Chapter 3 dealt extensively with image. There is also an increasing number of self-help books on the market dealing with how to create a positive first impression. If the manager has indicated that she is weak in this area, it could be well worth her while to learn more about projecting a positive image of herself.

Finding Mentors

Women often feel that if they work hard, their work will speak for itself and they will get ahead. Most of the research on successful managerial careers concludes that women need mentors. If women are to function effectively as managers, they must recognize that they need access to inner-circle support. Even women who have competence, skill, ability, and drive need a mentor.

Seeking a mentor is an active process. The manager can't afford to wait for a mentor to find her, but neither can she afford to pursue a mentor without first assessing her needs for progress. She must first have well-defined goals and a realistic assessment of her abilities. The mentor will be attracted to women who are capable, knowledgeable, visible, and interested in their careers.

FIGURE 11-7

DO I RECOGNIZE THAT A MENTOR CAN PROVIDE INVALUABLE SPONSORSHIP AND DO I KNOW HOW TO GO ABOUT SEEKING A MENTOR?

I am very weak in this area	I am somewhat weak in this area	I am strong in this area	I am very strong in this area

Managing Oneself

Chapter 5 on self-management dealt extensively with the management of a woman's career, time, and stress. Motivation was defined as the internal drive to accomplish a goal. Extensive analysis and aid were provided in helping the manager establish realistic long-term career goals. Her chances of finding career satisfaction increase dramatically by articulating and setting goals.

FIGURE 11-8

DO I FEEL THAT I KNOW WHAT MY GOALS ARE AT THIS POINT?

I am very weak in this area	I am somewhat weak in this area	I am strong in this area	I am very strong in this area

If the manager is very weak in the area of goal setting, we suggest she go back to Chapter 5 and review the goal-setting strategies covered there.

Time management also can aid the manager in effectively handling the pressures of the managerial job and accomplishing *more* in less time.

FIGURE 11-9

DO I FOLLOW THE PRINCIPLES OF TIME MANAGEMENT?

I am very weak in this area	I am somewhat weak in this area	I am strong in this area	I am very strong in this area

If the manager finds herself weak in the area of time management, we suggest she review Alan Lakein's *How to Get Control of Your Time and Your Life*, or any other time management book.[2] Basic to Lakein's system is learning to plan what one wants to do and then organizing one's use of time to get it done. Managing time, like managing stress, involves learning to manage one's own behavior.

FIGURE 11-10

AM I AWARE OF THE THINGS THAT CAUSE STRESS IN MY LIFE?

I am very weak in this area	I am somewhat weak in this area	I am strong in this area	I am very strong in this area

FIGURE 11-11

DO I HANDLE STRESS IN A POSITIVE MANNER BY MY DIET, SLEEP, REGULAR EXERCISE, AND LEISURE ACTIVITIES?

I am very weak in this area	I am somewhat weak in this area	I am strong in this area	I am very strong in this area

Developing Effective Communication Skills

Women often are socialized to speak in a polite way which emphasizes cooperation and compliance. While these speech patterns may be advantageous in some situations, in many business situations they will detract from the manager's influence and credibility. An awareness of word choice, voice intonation, hesitancy, and pitch is essential.

FIGURE 11-12

AM I AWARE OF THE CHARACTERISTICS OFTEN FOUND IN WOMEN'S SPEECH PATTERNS?

I am very weak in this area	I am somewhat weak in this area	I am strong in this area	I am very strong in this area

Being aware of the special communication problems women have is the first step to becoming an effective communicator. To strengthen their skills, women need to speak on an adult-to-adult level, own their feelings, and send specific, understandable, and concrete messages.

FIGURE 11-13

DO I KNOW HOW TO SEND CONCRETE MESSAGES ON AN ADULT-TO-ADULT LEVEL?

I am very weak in this area	I am somewhat weak in this area	I am strong in this area	I am very strong in this area

Handling Power and Politics

Utilizing power and politics in organizations is often an unpleasant but necessary chore for the woman who wants to be successful in a managerial career. Women's traditional periphery-type jobs, overprotective superiors, and lack of connections with the inside power holders often work as barriers to building adequate political power bases. Women managers can use feminine characteristics to their advantage, adopt appropriate masculine styles, and gain entry into political networks as strategies for overcoming these barriers. Their influence can also be enhanced by building power based on information, expertise, reference, coercion, rewards, and authority.

FIGURE 11-14

AM I AWARE OF THE INTRICACIES OF ORGANIZATIONAL POLITICS AND AM I IN COMMAND OF STRATEGIES TO BUILD AN EFFECTIVE POWER BASE?

I am very weak in this area	I am somewhat weak in this area	I am strong in this area	I am very strong in this area

Sometimes power must be applied in conflict situations for the good of both the individuals and organization involved. Confrontations are often required with disrespectful and counterproductive subordinates. At other times legitimate disagreements and conflicts arise that must be resolved in productive ways.

FIGURE 11-15

AM I SKILLED IN CONFRONTATION AND CONFLICT RESOLUTION?

I am very weak in this area	I am somewhat weak in this area	I am strong in this area	I am very strong in this area

Working Effectively with Groups

Working effectively with groups means being aware of the fundamentals of group dynamics and knowing how to apply this knowledge. Chapter 8 dealt extensively with the communication patterns, decision-making procedures, role behaviors, and emotional issues present in groups. It is important for a manager to take an active leadership role and encourage her group members to behave in ways which permit groups to function effectively. Productive managers are skilled in all of the various leadership and membership roles and share this knowledge with subordinates. Every member helps the group achieve its mission. A team member takes time to improve relationships with fellow workers and the supervisor.

FIGURE 11-16

AT THIS POINT IN MY CAREER, DO I KNOW HOW TO EFFECTIVELY WORK WITH GROUPS?

I am very weak in this area	I am somewhat weak in this area	I am strong in this area	I am very strong in this area

Dealing with Difficult Employees

Skill is needed when dealing with difficult employees. Effective managers recognize their own behavioral style and the behavioral styles of their employees. They adapt their behavioral style in order to avoid many of the potential conflicts that can arise with difficult employees.

FIGURE 11-17

AM I AWARE OF BEHAVIORAL STYLE CHARACTERISTICS OF THE EXPRESSIVE, THE DRIVER, THE ANALYTICAL, AND THE AMIABLE?

I am very weak in this area	I am somewhat weak in this area	I am strong in this area	I am very strong in this area

Being aware of behavioral style characteristics is the first step in dealing with difficult employees. When an employee and a manager with incompatible styles clash, much tension results; and the manager needs to know how to practice behavioral flexibility.

FIGURE 11-18

DO I KNOW HOW TO USE BEHAVIORAL FLEXIBILITY IN DEALING WITH DIFFICULT EMPLOYEES?

I am very weak in this area	I am somewhat weak in this area	I am strong in this area	I am very strong in this area

Hiring and Firing Employees

Two of the most important aspects of the staffing process are the hiring and firing of employees. When a manager does a good job of matching the right employee with the right job, everyone benefits. The interview is of key importance. When the manager asks good questions and makes a background check before she offers employment to an applicant, she can avoid costly mistakes.

FIGURE 11-19

WHEN HIRING A NEW EMPLOYEE, DO I STRUCTURE THE INTERVIEW TO SOLICIT VALUABLE INFORMATION IN AIDING ME TO MAKE A GOOD MATCH?

I am very weak in this area	I am somewhat weak in this area	I am strong in this area	I am very strong in this area

A PLAN TO FOLLOW

After the manager has evaluated herself using the various continuums presented in this chapter, she should have a good idea of where her strengths and weaknesses lie. Her ultimate goal is to move her *X*'s as far to the right on each continuum as she can. While this seems like an ambitious goal, Hauser said, "Shoot for the moon; even if you miss, you'll end up among the stars!"[3]

The manager has probably identified several areas that she would like to improve. She should select the one or two most important areas and focus on developing these skills. She should avoid trying to change too fast and keep a record of her progress.

The cycle of change given below is a helpful one in making the changes necessary to improve or sharpen a woman's management skills. It includes the following phases: (1) becoming aware of the need for change, (2) having the willingness or desire to change, (3) acquiring the knowledge needed to change, and (4) reinforcing new behavior.

Becoming Aware of the Need for Change

Growth begins with awareness. A manager may discover through this book and her self-assessment that she needs to change or improve. Other people may tell her that she needs to change some aspects of her behavior. Once she becomes aware of the need to change, she can begin to take initial steps toward where she wants to be.

Having the Willingness and Desire to Change

While awareness is the key to beginning the cycle of change, the manager's attitude toward that change is what makes her take action. The desire or willingness to plan for and follow through on a program to improve her skills is necessary. She should believe that change is possible for her and that she'll have an easier time accomplishing her goals.

Acquiring the Knowledge One Needs to Change

When the manager is aware of what she wants to work on and feels it will be beneficial, she has just completed an internal process.

Now is the time to look to others. She should seek expert knowledge, advice, and experience. This might mean finding a teacher, joining a professional group, or reading and teaching herself.

For example, suppose a manager decides that she wants to develop a more positive self-image. Her first step might be to visit the local bookstore or library and obtain a few self-help books. She reads the books and picks up several good ideas. But then she realizes that reading is not enough—she needs to talk with others who share the same goal. She may therefore enroll in a self-help class, join a consciousness-raising group, or just get together with two or three others who are concerned about improving their self-image. She should gain as much of the "how to" information as she can.

Many times the manager will need to rely on the feedback of others to tell her when she has really changed because often she will be too close to the process to tell. For example, a colleague may point out to her that she seldom accepts compliments. Whenever someone praises her work, the manager usually says that she didn't really do a very good job or that she realizes there was something that wasn't good about the job. Once she is aware of this tendency, she can practice saying "thank you" and accepting the compliment she rejected before. She can begin to see herself as a successful person who can accept recognition. Feedback from a colleague has helped her take another step toward an improved self-image.

Reinforcing One's New Behavior

When the manager finds herself exhibiting the type of behavior she wants to develop, or when someone mentions that she has changed, she should reward herself. The power of positive reinforcement works just as well for an individual as it does for an organization. The manager should reward herself for small, intermediate successes; they are just as important as the final step.

CONCLUSION

Regardless of the skill or behavior changes the manager is working on to improve herself, the plan outlined in this final chapter can work. One of the most exciting things about this plan is that it makes the manager compete against herself. She sets up her own standards and goals. She decides the kind of person she wants to be. The results can mean not only career advancement and financial benefits, but the development of strong, satisfying relationships with others. We wish her luck!

FOOTNOTES

1. Len Sperry, Douglas J. Mickelson, and Phillip L. Hunsaker, *You Can Make It Happen: A Guide to Self-Actualization and Organizational Change* (Reading, MA: Addison-Wesley Publishing Company, 1977).

2. Alan Lakein, *How to Get Control of Your Time and Your Life* (New York: Peter H. Wyden, 1973).

3. Leo Hauser, *Five Steps to Success* (Minneapolis, MN: Personal Dynamics Institute, 1980), p. 27.

SUGGESTED READINGS

Women Managers

Adams, L. *Effectiveness Training for Women*. New York: Wynden Books, 1979.

Bloom, Lynn A., Karen Coburn, and Joan Pearlman. *The New Assertive Woman*. New York: Dell, 1975.

Blotnick, Srully. *Otherwise Engaged: The Private Lives of Successful Career Women*. New York: Facts on File Publications, 1985.

Braham, James. "Women at the Top." *Industry Week* (March 4, 1985), pp. 106-108.

Carr-Ruffino, Norma. *The Promotable Woman—Becoming a Successful Manager*, 2d ed. Belmont, CA: Wadsworth Publishing Company, 1985.

Collins, Eliza G. C. *Dearest Amanda . . . An Executive's Advice to Her Daughter*. New York: Harper & Row, Publishers, 1984.

Fenn, Margaret. *In the Spotlight: Women Executives in a Changing Environment*. Englewood Cliffs, NJ: Prentice-Hall, 1980.

Harragan, Betty L. *Games Mother Never Taught You: Corporate Gamesmanship for Women*. New York: Warner Books, 1977.

Hennig, Margaret, and Anne Jardin. *The Managerial Woman*. Garden City, New York: Anchor Books, 1981.

Kanter, Rosabeth. *Men and Women of the Corporation*. New York: Basic Books, 1977.

Kleiman, Carol. *Women's Networks*. New York: Lippincott & Crowell, 1980.

Shapiro, Barry, and Evelyn Shapiro (eds.). *The Women Say/The Men Say*. New York: Dell, 1979.

Van Fleet, David D., and Julie G. Saurage. "Recent Research on Women in Management." *Akron Business and Economic Review* (Summer, 1984), pp. 15-24.

Management Skills

Colwill, Nina L. *The New Partnership: Women and Men in Organizations*. Palo Alto, CA: Mayfield Publishing Co., 1982.

Fenn, Margaret. *Making It in Management: A Behavioral Approach for Women Executives*. Englewood Cliffs, NJ: Prentice-Hall, 1978.

Hunsaker, Phillip L., and Anthony J. Alessandra. *The Art of Managing People*. Englewood Cliffs, NJ: Prentice-Hall, 1980.

Josefowitz, Natasha. *Paths to Power*. Reading, MA: Addison-Wesley, 1980.

Stewart, Nathaniel. *The Effective Woman Manager*. New York: John Wiley & Sons, 1978.

Stoner, James A. F. *Management*, 2d ed. Englewood Cliffs, NJ: Prentice-Hall, 1982.

Thompson, A., and M. Wood. *Management Strategies for Women or, Now That I'm Boss, How Do I Run This Place?* New York: Simon and Schuster, 1983.

Self-Image

Cho, Emily. *Looking Terrific*. New York: G. R. Putnam's Sons, 1978.

"Does What You Wear Tell Where You're Headed?" *U.S. News and World Report* (September 25, 1978), pp. 59, 62.

Molloy, John T. *The Woman's Dress for Success Book*. New York: Warner Books, 1977.

Thourlby, William. *You Are What You Wear—The Key to Business Success*. Kansas City: Sheed Andrews and McMeel, 1978.

Power and Politics

Brady, M., L. Dyer, and S. Parriott. *Woman Power!* Los Angeles: J. P. Taicher, Inc., 1981.

Connie, J. K. *The Woman's Guide to Management Success: How to Win Power in the Real Organizational World.* Englewood Cliffs, NJ: Prentice-Hall, 1978.

DuBrin, Andrew J. *Winning at Office Politics.* New York: Van Nostrand Reinhold, 1977.

Hart, Lois. *Moving Up! Women and Leadership.* New York: AMACOM, 1980.

Kennedy, Marilyn Moats. *Office Politics.* Chicago, IL: Follett Publishing Co., 1980.

Maccoby, Michael. *The Gamesman: The New Corporate Leaders.* New York: Simon and Schuster, 1976.

Work Groups

Douglas, Tom. *Basic Groupwork.* New York: International Universities Press, 1976.

Harrison, Albert A. *Individuals and Groups: Understanding Social Behavior.* Monterey, CA: Brooks/Cole, 1976.

Janis, Irving L. *Victims of Groupthink.* Boston: Houghton Mifflin Company, 1972.

Maier, Norman R. F. *Problem Solving and Creativity in Individuals and Groups.* Monterey, CA: Brooks/Cole, 1970.

Zonder, Alvin. *Groups at Work.* San Francisco: Jossey-Bass, 1977.

Communication

Bonville, Thomas G. *How to Listen—How to Be Heard.* Chicago: Nelson-Hall Inc., 1978.

Honey, Peter. *Face to Face: Business Communication for Results.* Englewood Cliffs, NJ: Prentice-Hall, 1978.

Huseman, Richard C., James M. Lahiff, and John D. Hutfield. *Interpersonal Communication in Organizations.* Boston: Holbrook Press, 1976.

Sussman, Lyle, and Paul D. Krivonos. *Communication for Supervisors and Managers*. Sherman Oaks, CA: Alfred Publishing Co., 1979.

Problem Solving

Elbing, Alvar. *Behavioral Decisions in Organizations*, 2d ed. Glenview, IL: Scott, Foresman and Company, 1978.

Harrison, E. Frank. *The Managerial Decision-Making Process*, 2d ed. Boston: Houghton Mifflin Company, 1981.

Levinson, Harr. "Management by Whose Objectives?" *Harvard Business Review*, Vol. 48 (May/June 1970), pp. 125-134.

Mentors

Fitt, L., and D. Newton. "When the Mentor Is a Man and the Protégée a Woman." *Harvard Business Review*, Vol. 59 (March/April, 1981), p. 56.

Kram, Kathy E. *Mentoring at Work: Developmental Relationships in Organizational Life*. Glenview, IL: Scott, Foresman and Company, 1984.

Sheehy, Gail. "The Mentor Connection: The Secret Link in Successful Women's Life." *New York Magazine* (April, 1976), pp. 14-23.

Career Development

Bolles, Richard N. *What Color Is Your Parachute? A Practical Manual for Job Hunters and Career Changers*. Berkeley, CA: Ten Speed Press, 1980.

Burack, E., M. Albrecht, and H. Seitler. *Growing: A Woman's Guide to Career Satisfaction*. Belmont, CA: Lifetime Learning Publications, 1980.

Byrne, John. "No Time to Waste." *Forbes* (May 6, 1985), pp. 110-114.

DuBrin, Andrew J. *Survival in the Office*. New York: Van Nostrand Reinhold, 1977. See Part V, "Managing Your Future."

Ekstrom, Ruth. "Women in Management: Factors Affecting Career Entrance and Advancement." *Selections*, Vol. II, No. 1 (1985), pp. 28-32.

Figler, Homer R. *Overcoming Executive Mid-Life Crisis*. New York: Wiley-Interscience, 1978.

Hall, Douglas T. *Careers in Organizations*. Santa Monica, CA: Goodyear Publishing Co., 1976.

Weiler, Nicholas W. *Reality and Career Planning: A Guide for Personal Growth*. Reading, MA: Addison-Wesley, 1977.

Zenger, John H., *et al. How to Work for a Living and Like It. A Career Planning Workbook*. Reading, MA: Addison-Wesley, 1977.

Time and Stress Management

Albrecht, K. *Stress and the Manager*. Englewood Cliffs, NJ: Prentice-Hall, 1979.

Bensahel, Jane G. "How to Get Home Unpursued by the Five Work Demons." *International Management* (March, 1978), pp. 55-56.

Benson, Herbert. *The Relaxation Response*. New York: William Morrow, 1975.

Burka, Jane, and L. Yuen. *Procrastination: Why You Do It, What to Do About It*. Reading, MA: Addison-Wesley, 1984.

Forbes, R. *Corporate Stress*. New York: Doubleday and Co., Inc., 1979.

Friedman, M., and R. Rosenman. *Type A Behavior and Your Heart*. New York: Fawcett Crest, 1974.

Gherman, E. *Stress and the Bottom Line*. New York: AMACOM, 1981.

Lakein, Alan. *How to Get Control of Your Time and Your Life*. New York: Peter H. Wyden, 1973.

GLOSSARY OF KEY TERMS

acceptance—a leader's ability to gain respect and win the confidence of others

accommodating—an approach to interpersonal conflict situations which consists of unassertive and cooperative behavior to satisfy the needs of the other person

accomplishment—the amount and quality of work produced mainly through the effective use of one's own time

adaptation techniques—methods of dealing with stress that solve a problem by modifying either the sources of stress or one's reactions to them

aggressor—a type of self-oriented role behavior by a group member who deflates others' status, attacks them or their values, and jokes in a barbed or semiconcealed way

Amiables—behavioral style of employees who are highly responsive, relatively unassertive, supportive, and reliable, but are slow to take action

Analyticals—behavioral style of employees who are persistent, systematic problem solvers and whose actions and decisions tend to be extremely cautious and slow

apologies—words that clutter or lengthen the speaker's requests or declarations and rob them of their focus and authority

attending—a term referring to the verbal, vocal, and visual messages that the active listener sends to the speaker

authentic feedback—feedback which consists of nonevaluative interpretations of how a person's or a group's behavior affects the feedback giver

avoider—a type of self-oriented role behavior by a group member who pursues special interests not related to the group's task, stays off the subject to avoid commitment, and prevents the group from facing up to any controversy

avoiding—an approach to interpersonal conflict situations which consists of unassertive and uncooperative behavior in order to diplomatically sidestep an issue, postpone it, or withdraw from a threatening situation

background check—an investigation verifying information obtained from a job candidate and collecting additional references

blocker—a type of self-oriented role behavior by a group member who disagrees and opposes beyond reason, resists stubbornly the group's wish, and uses a hidden agenda to thwart the group's movement

breadth of knowledge—a term referring to a person's ability to converse with others on topics outside of his or her particular area of expertise

career—the individually perceived sequence of attitudes and behaviors associated with work-related experiences and activities over the span of a person's life

Cinderella complex—the tendency of some women to sabotage their careers because of fear of success

clarifier—a type of task role behavior where a group member interprets ideas or suggestions, defines terms, and clarifies issues before the group

coercive power—the ability to punish subordinates if they do not conform to the manager's directives

collaborating—an approach to interpersonal conflict situations which consists of assertive and cooperative behavior in order to find a solution which fully satisfies the concerns of both parties

communication—a leader's ability to get through to people at all levels

communication process—a cycle which begins when one person sends a message to another with the intent of evoking a response and ends with the other person's response

comparable worth—the concept that jobs requiring comparable knowledge, skills, and abilities should pay at comparable levels

competing—an approach to interpersonal conflict situations which consists of assertive and uncooperative behavior in order to pursue one's concerns at another person's expense

compromiser—a type of maintenance role behavior where a group member offers a compromise that yields status to members involved in a conflict, admits error, and modifies a suggestion in the interest of group cohesion

compromising—an approach to interpersonal conflict situations which consists of splitting the difference, engaging in concessions, or seeking middle-ground positions in order to find a mutually acceptable middle ground which is expedient and partially satisfies both parties

conflict—a disagreement between two or more people where their concerns appear to be incompatible

consensus taker—a type of task role behavior where a group member asks to see if a group is nearing a decision and sends up a trial balloon to test a possible conclusion

consensus testing method—a method of decision making which consists of a genuine exploration to test for any opposition to an issue and to determine whether the opponents feel strongly enough to refuse to implement a decision

controlling—the management process of monitoring what is actually happening and correcting deviations from plans

coping techniques—methods of dealing with stress that involve helping a person put up with the problem

credibility—an important element in interpersonal communication evidenced by the belief of the receiver that the sender of a message is trustworthy

critical mass—more than two or three women included in large work groups in an effort to reduce stereotyping

delegation—the process of assigning responsibility for duties and tasks, and granting authority to perform them

depth of knowledge—a term referring to how well a person knows his or her partricular area of expertise

disclaimers—words or phrases which preface an opinion to protect the speaker from losing face but decrease the level of the speaker's influence

dominator—a type of self-oriented role behavior by a group member who asserts authority or superiority to manipulate the group, interrupts contributions of others, and controls the group by means of flattery or other forms of patronizing behavior

Drivers—behavioral style of employees who are firm with others and oriented toward productivity and concerned with bottom-line results

earned authority—the totality of one's power which is derived through competence, valued contributions, and individual character

empathy—the process of putting oneself into another's shoes so that one can understand matters from the other person's point of view

empty adjectives—words that connote little meaning and have a "fluffing" effect

encourager—a type of maintenance role behavior where a group member is friendly, warm, and responsive to others and indicates by facial expression or remark the acceptance of others' contributions

energizer—a type of task role behavior where a group member attempts to increase the quality and quantity of task behavior

expert power—the influence accorded to a manager who has superior knowledge, ability, or skill

Expressives—behavioral style of employees who are animated, intuitive, and lively but can be manipulative, impetuous, excitable, and spontaneous in making decisions

external recruitment sources—recruitment sources outside the organization

fact feedback—a type of feedback consisting of fact-finding questions that are meant to elicit specific data and information

feedback—the process of a receiver's telling the sender exactly what it is that the receiver heard being said and what the receiver thinks the meaning of the message is

feeling-feedback—a two-directional feedback by which the receiver makes a concerted effort to understand the feelings, emotions, and attitudes underlying the sender's message and projects to the sender that the message has gotten through

fillers—vocal sounds that signal the speaker's uncertainty and lack of preparation

flexibility—a leader's ability to cope with change and to adjust to the unexpected

follower—a type of maintenance role behavior where a group member serves as audience and passively goes along with the ideas of others

friendly helper style—an emotional style which consists of an acceptance of tender emotions and a denial of tough emotions

gatekeeper—a type of maintenance role behavior where a group member helps to keep communication channels open, facilitates the participation of others, and suggests procedures that permit the sharing of remarks

gatekeeping—the function of controlling the communication process so that everyone concerned has an equal chance to participate and be heard

good judgment—a leader's ability to reach sound conclusions based on all of the evidence available in a decision situation

handclasp—a method of decision making by which two people support each other to initiate a decision

harmonizer—a type of maintenance role behavior where a group member attempts to reconcile disagreements, reduces tension, and gets people to explore differences

hedging or modifying phrases—phrases that detract from the impact of a statement

helpmate—a feature of most female occupations which consists of assisting others in their work

help-seeker—a type of self-oriented role behavior by a group member who uses the group to solve personal problems which are unrelated to the group's goals

holding out—a blocking strategy in communication which prevents a decision or calls attention to a negative program that needs one's approval or participation to be successful

hypercorrect or excessively polite speech—speech that can give the sender an uptight image and that may be misinterpreted by the receiver

image—a term used to describe the picture a person projects to other people

influence—any psychological force which can cause a change in another person

information power—the influence a person has when he or she possesses information valuable to others who don't have it

information-seeker—a type of task role behavior where a group member asks for opinions or facts

informer—a type of task role behavior where a group member offers facts, gives expression of feelings, and gives opinions

initiative—a leader's ability to be a self-starter

initiator—a type of task role behavior where a group member proposes tasks, goals, or actions; defines group problems; and suggests procedures

internal recruitment sources—recruitment sources within the organization

interpersonal power—the ability to get another person to do something spontaneously that he or she would not have done necessarily

iron maiden—a female sex role which typecasts a woman as the tough type who acts in a task-oriented manner

job analysis—the preparation of a statement that depicts a job description and an acknowledgment of the desired background, experience, and personal characteristics of a person to fill that position

lateral transfer—transfer from one position to another at the same level or to a different location

leading—the management process of linking planned objectives and their achievement

legitimate power—power that is based on authority vested in an organizational position and accrues to the person who holds that position

listening—an intellectual and emotional process in which one integrates physical, emotional, and intellectual inputs in search of meaning

logical thinker style—a type of emotional style which consists of a denial of all emotion

majority-minority voting—a method of decision making by which the majority's suggestion rules over that of the minority

management—the process of planning, organizing, staffing, leading, and controlling the efforts of organizational members and using organizational resources to achieve stated organizational objectives

mentor—a senior person who undertakes to guide a younger person's career development

minority decision—a method of decision making by which a "together few" influence an "untogether whole"

mixed signals—the act of saying one thing while communicating something totally different through vocal intonation and body language

mother role—a female sex role based on the stereotyped assumption that women are nurturing and sympathetic listeners

multiple roles—a contributor to stress which consists of being responsible for many different kinds of activities

objectivity—a leader's ability to control personal feelings in an open-minded manner

observer-commentor—a type of maintenance role behavior where a group member comments on and interprets the group's internal process

office politics—the game of getting all the different human elements in an organization working for, rather than against, one

organizing—the management process of deciding who is going to do what, and how people and activities will be related

overload—a contributor to stress which consists of having too much to do in the time available

performance—a leader's ability to execute current duties exceptionally well

pet—a token role where the female is symbolically included in a management group like a mascot or cheerleader, but not as an equal or influential figure

planning—the management process of determining goals and how they are to be achieved

playgirl—a type of self-oriented role behavior by a group member who makes a display—in a flamboyant fashion—of her lack of involvement, "abandons" the group while remaining physically with it, and seeks recognition in ways not relevant to the group's task

plop—a method of decision making by which an assertive statement is followed by silence which, in effect, is a decision not to do what was previously suggested

polling method—a method of decision making by which everyone's thoughts about an issue are sought so that the initiator may use the results as if a decision had been reached

power—the means to get things done

primacy effect—the tendency of initial impressions to be preserved

procedural technician—a type of task role behavior where a group member records suggestions and distributes materials

Queen Bee—a successful woman who has made it to top management by working harder than most men and who keeps her hard-earned and well-deserved privileges for herself

questioning intonation—the tone at the end of a statement which neutralizes or eliminates the intended assertiveness of the statement

reality shock syndrome—a barrier to career development which consists of the disparity between initial job expectations and the hard realities of what the job actually entails

reality tester—a type of task role behavior where a group member makes critical analysis of an idea and tests it against some data to see if it would work

redundancy—a way to overcome communication barriers by using more than one channel of communication

referent power—the ability to cause others to imitate one's personal style or behavior because of their respect or liking for that person

relationship-related behavior—a leader's function which involves group maintenance to help the group operate more smoothly and feel good about its members

responding—a term referring to the active listener's giving feedback on the accuracy of the speaker's message and feelings, keeping the speaker talking, gathering more information, making the speaker feel understood, and getting the speaker to better understand the problems or concerns being discussed

reward power—the ability to compensate and give rewards to individuals who satisfactorily complete assigned tasks

role—behavior set that is aimed at accomplishing some objective

seductress—a female sex role in which a manager is typecast by male subordinates, peers, or superiors as a sex object who shares her attentions with many admirers

self-authorized agenda—a method of decision making by which an assertive statement is followed by self-initiated action

self-fulfilling prophecy—the phenomenon occurring when expectations are usually acted upon and confirmed

semistructured interview—a type of interview consisting of a limited set of prepared questions to ask of the job candidate

sensing—the ability to recognize the "silent" messages that a speaker is sending

servant trap—the situation in which a woman finds herself when her mentor asks her to do work that is more fitting for somone in a lower position

staffing—the management process of recruiting, placing, training, and developing organizational members

stereotypes—assumed differences, social conventions or norms, learned behaviors, attitudes, or expectations

strategic openness—disclosure of information when appropriate

stress—the rate of wear and tear on the body

stress management—the ability to manage the forces in a person's life rather than having these forces control the person

stressors—events or environments that are perceived as threatening and therefore produce stress

structured interview—a type of interview consisting of a prepared list of questions to ask of a job candidate from which the interviewer does not deviate

summarizer—a type of task role behavior where a group member pulls together related ideas, restates suggestions, and offers a decision or conclusion for the group to consider

tag question—question used after a declarative statement which automatically "passes the ball" from the sender of the message to the receiver

task-related behavior—a leader's function which is aimed at accomplishing the objectives of the work group

time waster—an oft-repeated event, incident, or situation which tends to eat into one's time

tough battler style—a type of emotional style which consists of an acceptance of tough emotions and a denial of tender emotions

transactional analysis—a method of explaining the interactions and communication between individuals based on the roles they assume

unstructured interview—a type of interview consisting of little preparation on the part of the interviewer other than a set of example topics

versatility—a term referring to a person's willingness and skill in adapting his or her behavior to best relate to other people

vertical transfer—promotion or demotion

INDEX

U, V, W, Y